I0025106

INTERNATIONAL DEVELOPMENT IN FOCUS

Boosting Productivity in Kazakhstan with Micro-Level Tools

Analysis and Policy Lessons

MARIANA IOOTTY, ASSET BIZHAN, AND PAULO G. CORREA

WORLD BANK GROUP

© 2022 International Bank for Reconstruction and Development / The World Bank
1818 H Street NW, Washington, DC 20433
Telephone: 202-473-1000; internet: www.worldbank.org
Some rights reserved

1 2 3 4 25 24 23 22

Books in this series are published to communicate the results of World Bank research, analysis, and operational experience with the least possible delay. The extent of language editing varies from book to book.

This work is a product of the staff of The World Bank with external contributions. The findings, interpretations, and conclusions expressed in this work do not necessarily reflect the views of The World Bank, its Board of Executive Directors, or the governments they represent. The World Bank does not guarantee the accuracy, completeness, or currency of the data included in this work and does not assume responsibility for any errors, omissions, or discrepancies in the information, or liability with respect to the use of or failure to use the information, methods, processes, or conclusions set forth. The boundaries, colors, denominations, and other information shown on any map in this work do not imply any judgment on the part of The World Bank concerning the legal status of any territory or the endorsement or acceptance of such boundaries.

Nothing herein shall constitute or be construed or considered to be a limitation upon or waiver of the privileges and immunities of The World Bank, all of which are specifically reserved.

Rights and Permissions

This work is available under the Creative Commons Attribution 3.0 IGO license (CC BY 3.0 IGO) http://creativecommons.org/licenses/by/3.0/igo. Under the Creative Commons Attribution license, you are free to copy, distribute, transmit, and adapt this work, including for commercial purposes, under the following conditions:

Attribution—Please cite the work as follows: Iootty, Mariana, Asset Bizhan, and Paulo G. Correa. 2022. *Boosting Productivity in Kazakhstan with Micro-Level Tools: Analysis and Policy Lessons.* International Development in Focus. Washington, DC: World Bank. doi:10.1596/978-1-4648-1910-0. License: Creative Commons Attribution CC BY 3.0 IGO

Translations—If you create a translation of this work, please add the following disclaimer along with the attribution: *This translation was not created by The World Bank and should not be considered an official World Bank translation. The World Bank shall not be liable for any content or error in this translation.*

Adaptations—If you create an adaptation of this work, please add the following disclaimer along with the attribution: *This is an adaptation of an original work by The World Bank. Views and opinions expressed in the adaptation are the sole responsibility of the author or authors of the adaptation and are not endorsed by The World Bank.*

Third-party content—The World Bank does not necessarily own each component of the content contained within the work. The World Bank therefore does not warrant that the use of any third-party-owned individual component or part contained in the work will not infringe on the rights of those third parties. The risk of claims resulting from such infringement rests solely with you. If you wish to re-use a component of the work, it is your responsibility to determine whether permission is needed for that re-use and to obtain permission from the copyright owner. Examples of components can include, but are not limited to, tables, figures, or images.

All queries on rights and licenses should be addressed to World Bank Publications, The World Bank Group, 1818 H Street NW, Washington, DC 20433, USA; e-mail: pubrights@worldbank.org.

ISBN: 978-1-4648-1910-0
DOI: 10.1596/978-1-4648-1910-0

Cover photo: © Turar Kazangapov / World Bank. Further permission required for reuse.
Cover design: Debra Naylor / Naylor Design Inc.

Contents

Boxes

Figures

Tables

Acknowledgments

This report was written by Mariana Iootty (senior economist), Asset Bizhan (consultant), and Paulo G. Correa (program leader). Xeniya Kirova (program assistant) provided administrative support. Donato De Rosa (lead country economist), Todor Milchevski (senior private sector specialist), and Sjamsu Rahardja (senior economist) provided excellent peer review comments.

This report was prepared as part of the Joint Economic Research Program (JERP) fiscal year 2020/21 task on "Technical Assistance to Support Productivity Growth in Kazakhstan—Micro Dynamics of Aggregate Productivity Growth." It builds on several analytical pieces produced under the JERP project by the following authors: Ana Cristina Alonso (consultant), Yeraly Beksultan (senior private sector specialist), Asset Bizhan (consultant), Cesar Borja (analyst), Elwyn Davies (senior economist), José N. Franco (researcher, Polytechnic University of Madrid, Spain), Mariana Iootty (senior economist), Harald Jedlicka (senior private sector specialist), Nona Karalashvili (economist), Adina Mamrayeva (consultant), Dayo Ojaleye (consultant), Gaukhar Ospanova (private sector specialist), Zenia Rogatschnig (consultant), Luis Rubalcaba (professor of economics, University of Alcalá, Spain, and consultant), Yassin Sabha (consultant), Alena Sakhonchik (analyst), Stefka Slavova (lead economist), Shawn Tan (senior economist), Dea Tusha (consultant), Kohei Ueda (consultant), and Erik Van der Marel (professor, Université Libre de Bruxelles, and consultant).

These analytical pieces were peer reviewed by the following World Bank staff: Mikhail Bunchuk (senior digital development specialist), Francisco Campos (senior economist), Maciej Drozd (economist), Sevara Melibaeva (senior transport economist), Juan Navas-Sabater (lead digital development specialist), Ivan Anton Nimac (lead private sector specialist), Antonio Nunez (infrastructure program leader), and Ifeyinwa Uchenna Onugha (senior private sector specialist).

The team is grateful to the Economic Sectors Development Department of the Ministry of National Economy of Kazakhstan, the Economic Research Institute, the Kazakhstan Industry and Export Center (QazIndustry), and other public and private sector counterparts for useful comments and suggestions.

The team would also like to thank Ilias Skamnelos (practice manager) and Jean-François Marteau (country manager) for overall guidance.

About the Authors

Asset Bizhan is a private sector specialist based in the World Bank's Country Office in Kazakhstan. He has been engaged in several private sector development projects in the Caucasus, Central Asia, and Western Africa and has coauthored reports on private sector development and development of innovation ecosystems in Central Asia and Kazakhstan. Before joining the World Bank, Bizhan worked as senior risk manager at the private Temir Bank and as a market analyst at the international telecom vendor Alcatel-Lucent. He holds a master's degree in economics from the George Washington University (Washington, DC) and a bachelor's degree in economics from KIMEP University (Almaty, Kazakhstan).

Paulo G. Correa is the World Bank's lead economist and program leader for Equitable Growth, Finance, and Institutions in the Comoros, Madagascar, Mauritius, Mozambique, and the Seychelles. He led the preparation of this report between 2019 and 2020, when he was the lead economist for the Finance, Competitiveness, and Innovation Global Practice in the Europe and Central Asia Region. Correa has worked for the World Bank for 20 years, assisting governments with designing and implementing reforms to promote private investment, productivity, and inclusive growth and to reduce poverty. Before joining the World Bank, he worked in Brazil's Ministry of Finance, to which he returned between 2015 and 2016 to serve as Secretary of Economic Affairs. Correa holds a master's degree in economics from the University of Western Ontario.

Mariana Iootty is a senior economist at the World Bank working in the Finance, Competitiveness, and Innovation Global Practice in the Europe and Central Asia Region. Her main area of expertise is the microeconomic foundations of economic development and firm performance. Iootty is an economist by training and has been with the World Bank for 12 years. During this time, she has led analytical and advisory projects on private sector development, productivity growth, trade competitiveness, economic diversification, ex post evaluation of business support programs, innovation, and entrepreneurship in several countries. She has also led and contributed to the design of multisectoral lending operations and authored technical papers for regional flagship publications in the Europe and Central Asia, East Asia and Pacific, and Latin America and the Caribbean Regions. Before joining the World Bank, Iootty was a tenured professor of microeconomics and econometrics and a consultant to several private and public sector entities in Brazil; she was also a visiting fellow at the University of Reading (England). She holds a PhD in economics from the Federal University of Rio de Janeiro.

Executive Summary

INTRODUCTION

Productivity growth is at the forefront of Kazakhstan's economic strategy. The Strategic Development Plan of the Republic of Kazakhstan until 2025 lists productivity growth as one of the critical drivers of economic transformation to lift Kazakhstan into the top 30 most developed countries by 2050.

This report summarizes work under the client-funded fiscal year 2020/21 Joint Economic Research Program Technical Assistance to Support Productivity Growth in Kazakhstan. The work explored firm-level data to detect the causes of low productivity growth and identify policies to boost productivity performance in the country. It empirically studied administrative firm-level data shared by the government of Kazakhstan to deepen the understanding of the microeconomic dynamics and main drivers of aggregate productivity growth in the country. The analysis gave rise to a set of policy recommendations to boost aggregate productivity growth, especially outside the oil sector. The task encompassed three components: (1) "Setting the stage—Understanding microfoundations of low-productivity growth," (2) "Government interventions and market contestability," and (3) "Innovation, entrepreneurship and SMEs [small and medium enterprises]." The current document summarizes the main findings of all deliverables produced under these three components and highlights the key policy recommendations, extracted from these deliverables, for boosting productivity growth in the country.

BACKGROUND AND CONTEXT

Kazakhstan is an upper-middle-income, resource-rich economy that experienced substantial growth in the services sector over the past two decades. As a large oil exporter in Central Asia, Kazakhstan has successfully leveraged its oil resources to reduce poverty and increase shared prosperity. Following a pattern common to natural resource–based economies, robust revenue inflows from the oil sector bid up demand for nontradables at the expense of other exportable goods (manufactured goods, for example). As a result, the services sector—especially nontradable services—has increased its share of the economy from 49.4 percent of GDP in 2001 to 55.8 percent in 2019.

Productivity in Kazakhstan has been declining in recent years. Kazakhstan experienced strong total factor productivity (TFP) growth during the early 2000s, with TFP contributing 6 percentage points, on average, to annual GDP growth. The global financial crisis had a pronounced effect on both the scale and the nature of productivity growth in Kazakhstan. This period of high productivity in the early 2000s was followed by a decline in 2008–09, a productivity resumption (at a much lower level) in 2010–13, and declining productivity in 2015–16, with the main driver of GDP growth being the capital base. The decrease in TFP growth since the 2010s has mirrored a decline in oil prices and reflected an expansion of jobs at the low-value end of the spectrum in manufacturing, services, and agriculture.

Kazakhstan must accelerate productivity growth to escape the middle-income trap and avoid decelerating growth of GDP per capita. Accelerating productivity growth will require breaking the commodity cycle, which will only happen with an expanding productive and competitive private sector, diversified away from minerals.

SUMMARY OF EMPIRICAL FINDINGS

An analysis of firm-level data confirms that TFP growth has been muted in both manufacturing and services, with a modest expansion in the most recent years. After recovering from the global financial crisis in 2007–09, Kazakhstan's TFP growth started to slow in the early 2010s. Productivity growth declined even more with the economic crisis of 2014 following the fall in oil prices and a major devaluation, which weakened domestic demand and contributed to a gradual deterioration of potential output. TFP declined between 2010 and 2015 in both manufacturing and services. However, in more recent years, TFP growth has started to bounce back, albeit at a modest pace, possibly driven by the recovery in commodity prices. Between 2015 and 2018, TFP grew by 1.1 percent in the manufacturing sector and 0.4 percent in the services sector.

The regions and activities with the highest TFP growth are related to mining. In the regions with the highest TFP growth, mining activities play a crucial role in value added and employment. Similarly, the activities with the highest TFP growth are nontradable sectors, including transport and storage and mining itself.

Kazakhstan's modest productivity performance in the recent past, in both manufacturing and services, has resulted from muted performance across all three key components of productivity growth. There are three mechanisms by which aggregate productivity growth can improve: improvement in firm capabilities (within-firm productivity growth), improvement in factor allocation (between-firm productivity growth), and productive entry and exit of firms from the market (business dynamism). Results based on firm-level data show that Kazakhstan is underperforming in all three areas. Poland, by comparison, had allocative efficiency of 15–21 percent in the years after it made the transition to a market economy.

Business entry in Kazakhstan's formal private sector is still insufficient, despite a reduction in costs to start a business. According to Doing Business data, the cost to open a business shrank from 8.6 percent of income per capita in

2016/17 to 0.3 percent of income per capita in 2019/20. Moreover, the entry rate of firms into the formal sector in Kazakhstan increased between 2006 and 2018. However, Kazakhstan's new firm entry rate is much lower than the regional averages in Europe and Central Asia.

Likewise, formal private firms do not grow as they age, reflecting a stagnant private sector. For example, retail firms of any age in Kazakhstan employ about 14 workers, but in Chile, those 0–10 years old employ 33 workers, those 11–20 years old employ 76 workers, and those more than 20 years old employ 110 workers, on average.

The fact that private sector firms in Kazakhstan struggle to grow suggests that their productivity is not rewarded, reflecting a distortive operating environment that interferes with the allocation of resources toward firms with higher productivity and growth potential. Resource allocation does not occur naturally when the business environment is distorted such that it allows underperforming firms to survive or fails to provide incentives for efficient firms to grow.

All these empirical results point to a common conclusion: Kazakhstan has room to leverage all three sources of productivity growth (that is, improving firm capabilities, boosting factor allocation toward more productive firms, and enhancing productive entry and exit). A comprehensive productivity policy needs to encompass all three components of productivity growth.

Increasing productivity growth becomes even more critical in the context of the COVID-19 (coronavirus) pandemic and the climate change crisis. COVID-19 recovery programs and the strategies that will come from them are opportunities not only to regain lost economic ground but also to accelerate the green transition of the Kazakhstani economy. And accelerating the transition to a green economy is, in turn, an opportunity to tune the economy for high-productivity growth.

SUMMARY OF POLICY DIAGNOSIS

The analysis reveals four main policy areas for Kazakhstan to address to boost productivity. They are (1) competition distortions in product markets due to state involvement in the economy, (2) business support policies that prioritize firm survival rather than productivity growth, (3) the lack of a well-functioning institutional framework to attract productivity-enhancing foreign direct investment (FDI), and (4) several constraints on innovation (underinvestment in research and development [R&D], a fragmented national innovation system, and weak science-industry links).

Product market regulation in Kazakhstan (as it appears on the books) is considerably more restrictive to competition than the regulatory frameworks in Eastern European countries and the Organisation for Economic Co-operation and Development average. Most of these restrictions come from distortions induced by state involvement in the economy, first and foremost through a high level of direct state involvement via state-owned enterprises (SOEs). SOEs compete on uneven terms with the private sector, and there are restrictive public procurement policies. The continued use of price control mechanisms may also distort workably competitive markets. Barriers to competition in network sectors—in particular transport and telecommunications—are also sizable. Limited third-party access to essential infrastructure, other regulatory barriers to entry, and heavy public ownership play key roles in protecting incumbents, with high costs for the economy. In the telecommunications sector, barriers to competition are hindering digital infrastructure. In the transportation sector, barriers to competition are increasing connectivity costs.

Although the government of Kazakhstan has been deploying large-scale business support programs—most of them targeting micro, small, and medium enterprises (MSMEs)—they primarily provide incentives that promote firm survival rather than increase firm productivity. As a result, dynamism in the MSME sector remains low. The total budget of business support programs implemented in recent years exceeds 4.5 trillion Kazakhstani tenge, roughly 6.6 percent of GDP in 2020. Nevertheless, the productivity performance of formal private MSMEs in Kazakhstan is low and has been deteriorating. MSMEs in Kazakhstan may be failing to realize the trade gains from export activities. Furthermore, innovation, adoption of digital solutions, and multiple general capabilities of private MSMEs are underdeveloped compared with the Europe and Central Asia region average. Part of this underperformance is because existing support programs do not encompass explicit incentives for MSME productivity growth. Instead, they contain implicit disincentives for MSMEs to enter new geographic and product markets that could offer higher productivity payoffs. The COVID-19 crisis highlights the need to calibrate business support programs to tackle deeper structural challenges while helping rebuild better so that a stronger, greener, and more inclusive economy flourishes. In this context, refocusing business support policies from firm survival to higher dynamism and productivity growth is crucial.

Kazakhstan is not making the most of the benefits that FDI can bring to host countries, including productivity-enhancing benefits. FDI firms in Kazakhstan—like those in most countries—enjoy a productivity premium over their domestic peers and outperform domestic companies in technology innovation and product and service innovation. However, more than 50 percent of Kazakhstan's FDI is in the extractives sector, and more than 60 percent of FDI inflows are attached to commodity global value chains, which hinders productivity spillovers. Moreover, the COVID-19 crisis has negatively affected FDI flows globally. The oil and gas sectors are expected to be particularly affected, putting Kazakhstan at high risk for COVID-19–related effects on FDI. In this context, increasing investment promotion activity and creating a well-functioning FDI institutional framework to attract productivity-enhancing FDI are critical. Multiple institutions are involved in investment policy formulation and execution in Kazakhstan, and their relationships and collaboration leave room for improvement.

Kazakhstan is underinvesting in R&D and lags behind its peers in innovativeness, partly because of the fragmentation of the policy delivery structure and the absence of robust mechanisms to support science-industry collaboration, hampering firm productivity growth. Kazakhstan's gross expenditure on R&D as a share of GDP is systematically less than what would be expected given its level of economic development and is much lower than in other natural resource–intensive countries, including Australia and Canada. In addition, despite having a relatively large number of organizations and personnel engaged in R&D, Kazakhstan's number of patents—a proxy for innovativeness—significantly lags behind peer countries. Moreover, only 2.1 percent of formal private firms in Kazakhstan spend anything on R&D, about four times lower than the Europe and Central Asia region average. The national innovation system remains fragmented, with a lack of coordination among numerous actors that constrains opportunities for science-industry collaboration and thereby hampers productivity growth. Risk aversion among state institutions has limited government efforts to encourage innovation by nurturing start-ups.

SUMMARY OF RECOMMENDATIONS

The underlying work resulted in the overall set of policy recommendations summarized in table ES.1. In considering these recommendations, it is essential to keep in mind that productivity has many drivers, but this analysis focuses on the selected set studied under the Joint Economic Research Program. In particular, the study looks at the micro-foundations of productivity growth and focuses on selected policy areas related to competition, regulation, and FDI (which directly influence distortions in the operating environment of firms), and innovation, entrepreneurship, and MSMEs (which facilitate the upgrading of firms' capabilities). These are important drivers, and the policy recommendations are worth pursuing in their own right. Indeed, they span multiple policy areas and stakeholders, and their implementation will require efficient coordination and political processes of varying complexity and cost. Nevertheless, a comprehensive analysis of productivity growth would be incomplete without looking at physical and human capital, the macroeconomic environment, and other areas not covered here.

TABLE ES.1 Policy options to boost productivity growth in Kazakhstan: A summary

A. REMOVING COMPETITION DISTORTIONS THAT OBSTRUCT THE REALLOCATION OF PRODUCTIVE RESOURCES TOWARD THE MOST EFFICIENT FIRMS AND THAT PREEMPT PRODUCTIVITY GAINS

KEY AREAS	TIMELINE	RESPONSIBLE ACTOR(S)	KEY IMPLEMENTATION CHALLENGES
Economywide			
Foster competitive neutrality principles in markets by (1) requiring a clear separation between commercial and noncommercial activities of SOEs, (2) mandating that SOEs earn rates of return comparable to private sector competitors, (3) limiting conflicting roles of the state as regulator and operator in certain sectors, and (4) ensuring full debt and regulatory liability of SOEs.	Short term	MoF, MNE	The process of fostering competitive neutrality principles may be hampered by the presence of high-ranking government officials on SOEs' boards, risking political interference in SOE operations to prevent price and tariff hikes for goods and services that have been previously cross-subsidized.
Consider reducing the use of noncompetitive methods for awarding procurement contracts, ensuring fairness and transparency.	Short term	MoF	Because procurement in major SOEs is regulated by a separate law and SOEs' internal rules, the key challenge is the lack of accountability of SOEs' management.
Consider limiting the scope of price controls to market failure scenarios and for a limited time while gradually removing unnecessary price controls in industries without a clear market failure to be addressed.	Medium term	MNE line ministries	The lack of strong political championship and the lack of broad public discussion and consensus-building on price liberalization are key challenges.
Sector specific			
Telecommunications			
Consider unbundling the vertically integrated incumbent SOEs. For instance, • Unbundling the two mobile operators (Mobile Telecom-Service LLP and Kcell JSC) that had originally been separate companies and preparing them for privatization • Unbundling Kazakhtelecom into a wholesale arm and a retail arm to introduce more transparency and eliminate internal cross-subsidies.	Short term	Prime Minister's Office	Diseconomies of scale may cause higher average cost of mobile communication services. The unbundling may result in higher capital and operational expenditures by the two operators. Political economy issues may arise because the unbundling may lead to broadband tariff hikes in the short term.
Consider strengthening the regulatory authority or separating the sector regulator from the policy-making ministry. For instance, passing legislation to strengthen the regulatory authority for the telecommunications sector (Telecommunications Committee of the MDDIAI) and separate the sector regulator (Telecommunications Committee of the MDDIAI) from the policy-making ministry (the MDDIAI).	Medium term	Competition Protection and Development Agency, MDDIAI, Parliament	Because decisions of a regulator may have significant economic impacts on various stakeholders, strengthening the authority of the telecom regulator may evoke resistance from business entities and public institutions. As a result, this may become a lengthy political process as well as bring about transaction costs.

(Continued)

TABLE ES.1, *continued*

A. REMOVING COMPETITION DISTORTIONS THAT OBSTRUCT THE REALLOCATION OF PRODUCTIVE RESOURCES TOWARD THE MOST EFFICIENT FIRMS AND THAT PREEMPT PRODUCTIVITY GAINS

KEY AREAS	TIMELINE	RESPONSIBLE ACTOR(S)	KEY IMPLEMENTATION CHALLENGES
Telecommunications			
Consider removing legislative bottlenecks preventing private companies from accessing key input infrastructure. For instance, • Removing existing access restrictions to underutilized fiber-optic networks managed by private real estate management companies, public utilities, and telecom operators with significant market power, for example, by introducing open-access regulations to manage conditions of access, capacity allocation, access pricing, nondiscrimination, and dispute resolution	Short term	MDDIAI	Legislative bottlenecks that prevent co-deployment of telecom infrastructure along with nontelecom utilities through harmonization of a number of laws (governing telecom, energy, transport, construction, utilities sectors) and related bylaws and rules. The key challenge is the political process of amending the laws on communications and national security that limit entry to the cross-border connectivity market.
• Removing entry restrictions in the cross-border connectivity market • Passing regulations to encourage infrastructure sharing of fiber-optic backbone capacity, passive and active infrastructure, and access to essential facilities, including those managed by public utilities (for example, stipulating indiscriminate access of telecom operators to premises of real estate objects in urban areas).	Short term Medium term		The requirement for better coordination between the MDDIAI, regional authorities, and utility and construction companies might be a time- and resource-consuming process.
Transport			
Consider strengthening vertical separation (in particular, well-enforced accounting separation) of KTZ's operations along the value chain to avoid cross-subsidizing or transfer of funds into segments open to competitors.	Short term	Committee on Regulation of Natural Monopolies under the MNE, MIID	Potential resistance to the separation referring to diseconomies of scope and efficiency loss.
Consider strengthening the regulatory authority or separating the sector regulator from the policy-making ministry. For instance, passing legislation to strengthen the regulatory authority for the transport sector (Transport Committee of MIID) and separate the sector regulator (Transport Committee of MIID) from the policy-making ministry (MIID).	Medium term	Competition Protection and Development Agency, MIID, Parliament	Because decisions of a regulator may have significant economic impacts on various stakeholders, strengthening the authority of the transport regulator may evoke resistance from business entities and public institutions. As a result, this may become a lengthy political process as well as bring about transaction costs.
Consider removing legislative bottlenecks preventing private companies from accessing key input infrastructure, for instance, separating the coordination and organization function of access to the mainline railway network from KTZ Express's freight-forwarding business.	Medium term	MIID	Ensuring de facto separation of coordination function of KTZ Express may be challenging without independence of the sector regulator from MIID or divestiture of KTZ Express from KTZ (or both).

(Continued)

TABLE ES.1, continued

	B. RESHAPING BUSINESS SUPPORT POLICIES TO PRIORITIZE FIRM PRODUCTIVITY GROWTH RATHER THAN FIRM SURVIVAL		
KEY AREAS	TIMELINE	RESPONSIBLE ACTOR(S)	KEY IMPLEMENTATION CHALLENGES
Conduct a public expenditure review of existing MSME support programs to scale up successful ones and redesign or discontinue those that do not work.	Short term	MNE, MoF, MIID, regional akimats,a Bureau of National Statistics	Public expenditure review will require a comprehensive set of data on inputs and outputs of at least five major support programs. Because the programs were launched as far back as 2010 under overlapping and uncoordinated initiatives, attribution of programs' activities to beneficiaries' performance poses a major challenge.
Move from business support programs that focus only on size-based criteria to programs that provide incentives for firm growth and productivity increases. Consider revisiting the targeting criteria applied by current business support programs so that MSME growth, rather than survival, is indeed prioritized.	Short term	MNE, MoF, MIID, Prime Minister's Office, Administration of the President, Parliament, National Bank	Because the existing support programs and size-based policies are "too large to close," the transition to new support programs with fundamentally different development objectives will need to be gradual to allow MSMEs to adjust. Retaining political championship during this period might be challenging.
Consider redesigning MSME support policies to connect with broader policies. For instance, • *Connecting MSMEs to green growth strategy.* Consider developing proactive instruments to help MSMEs adapt to new environmental regulations and to create, adopt, and sell low-carbon and energy-efficient technologies or services through the development of information-sharing platforms, implementation of green financing mechanisms, and introduction of "green" certification criteria for public procurement purposes. • *Connecting MSMEs to digital transition.* Consider implementing specific measures to accelerate the adoption of digital technologies by MSMEs (for example, provide one-time marketing consultancy or training vouchers, help MSMEs access cloud computing and purchase cloud technology, promote awareness campaigns to decrease distrust toward e-commerce practices, and provide comprehensive information and guidelines to MSMEs on regulations related to e-commerce in Kazakhstan and its key trading partners).	Medium term	MNE	Coordination of many stakeholders involved in redesigning and connecting MSME policies with broader policies may present a major challenge. A particular challenge is building MSMEs' capacity to adopt digital technologies and the absence of connectivity in rural areas and small towns.
Strengthen the institutional framework to deliver MSME policies. For instance, • *Strengthen coordination mechanisms* (public to public). Consider consolidating programs in a single document—a consolidated MSME strategy—and outline an action plan with clear objectives and responsibilities of different state bodies in charge of program implementation. • *Encourage proactive involvement* of regional authorities, the private sector, and other relevant institutions (universities, research centers, and so on) in the design and implementation of MSME policies.	Medium term	MNE	Coordination of a large number of stakeholders involved in redesigning and subsequent implementation of revised MSME policies may present a major challenge.

(Continued)

TABLE ES.1, *continued*

C. UNLOCKING OPPORTUNITIES FOR FDI IN NONEXTRACTIVE SECTORS			
KEY AREAS	**TIMELINE**	**RESPONSIBLE ACTOR(S)**	**KEY IMPLEMENTATION CHALLENGES**
Review sector priorities for FDI attraction; identify a small number (three to five) of high-value target sectors for proactive investment promotion that are aligned with Kazakhstan's development objectives in the changing global environment.	Short term	Kazakh Invest, Investment Committee, MFA, MNE	Identifying target sectors would be best done by conducting a sector scan, which would require sector expertise and analytical capacity. The number of entities involved in investment policy and promotion may present a challenge for coordinating and agreeing upon target sectors.
Revise the mandate of Kazakh Invest to focus mostly on investment promotion as well as on policy advocacy and matchmaking between FDI and the local private sector (and not or business regulatory functions).	Short term	Investment Committee, MFA, MNE, Kazakh Invest	Streamlining the mandate of Kazakh Invest will require moving business regulatory functions to another government agency or institution, which will in turn need to organize the administration of these additional functions.
Introduce key performance indicators to Kazakh Invest for measuring the success of its investment promotion efforts.	Medium term	Investment Committee, MFA, MNE, Kazakh Invest	Introducing key performance indicators will benefit from baseline data and historical information on key targets, which may not be easily accessible.
Establish an effective national-subnational framework for coordinating the investment promotion activities of Kazakh Invest and the local-level entities (akimats).	Medium term	Kazakh Invest, akimats, Investment Committee	The capacity of different akimats to undertake investment promotion and facilitation activities may vary greatly, which could result in differing levels of engagement with Kazakh Invest and the need for additional local capacity.
Enhance institutional coordination mechanisms between policy makers (ministry) and implementing agencies (Kazakh Invest) for Kazakhstan's investment attraction and retention policies.	Medium term	Investment Committee, MFA, MNE, Kazakh Invest	Having different ministries involved in policy formulation and implementation, in addition to having a committee under which the investment agency works, means that the development of robust coordination mechanisms or the reorganization of existing reporting structures will be required to create a coherent structure.

(Continued)

xx | BOOSTING PRODUCTIVITY IN KAZAKHSTAN WITH MICRO-LEVEL TOOLS

TABLE ES.1, *continued*

	D. BOOSTING R&D AND INNOVATION TO MAXIMIZE THE IMPACT ON PRODUCTIVITY		
KEY AREAS	**TIMELINE**	**RESPONSIBLE ACTOR(S)**	**KEY IMPLEMENTATION CHALLENGES**
Establish a trusted platform for the impartial monitoring and evaluation of the effectiveness of the national innovation system and different public and private initiatives within it. For instance, establish an Innovation Observatory, envisaged under the Fostering Productive Innovation Project, as an efficient science, technology, and innovation policy coordination tool.	Medium term	Prime Minister's Office	The establishment of an independent policy coordinator delineated from multiple interest groups requires strong central government ownership and leadership.
Expand MSMEs' capabilities to develop or adapt innovations by improving management consulting services to MSMEs. For instance, • Develop a network of capable technology transfer offices at public research organizations and universities • Scale up existing technology commercialization support instruments based on the experience of the Fostering Productive Innovation Project (that is, development of the institute of technology brokers).	Medium term	MoES, MDDIAI	Building up commercialization capacity of the existing network of technology transfer offices is a key challenge because of the limited knowledge of and experience in collaborating with industry and technology commercialization.
Spread the adoption of productive technologies by scaling up existing pilots of innovative consortium activities. For instance, expand and replicate the innovative consortium activities introduced under the World Bank–financed Fostering Productive Innovation Project.	Short term	MDDIAI	The scaling up of the existing consortia grant program may be hampered by the dismantling of the existing independent selection board and the lack of stable and long-term funding from the public budget.
Close the financing gaps for technology start-ups and combine early-stage financing with nonfinancial support. For instance, develop a mechanism for early-stage financing of start-ups and pipeline-building for venture investments in later-stage entities, based on the experience of the Early-Stage Venture Fund under the Fostering Productive Innovation Project.	Medium term	MDDIAI, Baiterek Holding	Funding for early stages of research commercialization (such as preparing proofs-of-concept, prototyping, and so on) is underprovided by the private sector. Therefore, it is important to develop a sound mechanism for early-stage financing. To date, not a single early-stage venture capital fund operates in the country.
Ensure that selection of R&D teams and start-ups within the framework of support programs is based on commercialization potential. For instance, strengthen mechanisms that ensure merit-based selection of research proposals, specifically by enhancing the engagement of the private sector and industry in formulating research priorities for public research organizations at the level of national scientific councils.	Short term	MoES and other line ministries (MIID, MoH, MoA, MoE)	Currently, the challenge is to link national scientific council decisions to industry needs given that there is no real industry interest in the research areas because of the lack of dialogue with the private sector.

Source: World Bank.

Note: FDI = foreign direct investment; KTZ = Kazakhstan Temir Zholy; MDDIAI = Ministry of Digital Development, Innovation and Aerospace Industry; MFA = Ministry of Foreign Affairs; MIID = Ministry of Industry and Infrastructural Development; MNE = Ministry of National Economy; MoA = Ministry of Agriculture; MoE = Ministry of Energy; MoES = Ministry of Education and Science; MoF = Ministry of Finance; MoH = Ministry of Healthcare; MSMEs = micro, small, and medium enterprises; R&D = research and development; SOE = state-owned enterprise.

a. Regional akimats are governments of regions, of the capital city, and of cities of republican significance.

Abbreviations

COVID-19	coronavirus
FDI	foreign direct investment
GDP	gross domestic product
GVC	global value chain
JERP	Joint Economic Research Program
JSC	joint-stock company
KTZ	Kazakhstan Temir Zholy
LLP	limited liability partnership
MDDIAI	Ministry of Digital Development, Innovation and Aerospace Industry
MIID	Ministry of Industry and Infrastructural Development
MNC	multinational corporation
MNE	Ministry of National Economy
MoES	Ministry of Education and Science
MSMEs	micro, small, and medium enterprises
NIS	national innovation system
OECD	Organisation for Economic Co-operation and Development
PMR	Product Market Regulation
PRO	public research organization
R&D	research and development
SK	Samruk-Kazyna National Welfare Fund
SMEs	small and medium enterprises
SOE	state-owned enterprise
T	Kazakhstani tenge
TFP	total factor productivity
TFPR	revenue-based measures of total factor productivity
UNCTAD	United Nations Conference on Trade and Development
US$	United States dollar

1 Background and Context

INTRODUCTION

Kazakhstan is an upper-middle-income, resource-rich economy that has experienced substantial growth in the services sector over the past two decades. As a large oil exporter in Central Asia, Kazakhstan has successfully leveraged its oil resources to reduce poverty and increase shared prosperity: the proportion of the population living on less than US$3.2 a day decreased from 29.8 percent in 2001 to 0.2 percent in 2018.[1] Following a pattern common to natural resource–based economies, robust revenue inflows from the oil sector bid up demand for nontradables at the expense of other exportable goods (manufactured goods, for example). As a result, the services sector—especially nontradable services—has increased its share of the economy. Services grew from 49.4 percent of GDP in 2001 to 55.8 percent in 2019. Over the same period, agriculture declined from 6.2 percent of GDP to 5.3 percent, and manufacturing fell from 16.4 percent of GDP to 13.1 percent. The services sector accounts for 66.8 percent of total employment, the agriculture sector accounts for 13.5 percent, and the manufacturing sector accounts for 6.7 percent. The wholesale and retail trade and education segments are the largest employers in the services sector, accounting for 16.3 percent and 12.7 percent of total employment, respectively.

After a decade of robust results, Kazakhstan's GDP growth has steadily fallen since the global financial crisis, with a recent uptick in 2017 and 2019. Between 2000 and 2010, Kazakhstan's economy grew by an annual average of 8 percent, placing the country among the world's top 20 most rapidly expanding economies (figure 1.1). Strong growth in this period, particularly in the oil and gas sectors, and some economywide reforms in the early 2000s drove significant welfare gains as real wages surged. Between 2000 and 2010, GDP per capita in Kazakhstan also converged noticeably with that of the United States: as of 2010, Kazakhstan's GDP per capita was nearly 36.5 percent of the United States', considerably higher than in 2000 (12.4 percent).[2] However, this process slowed in the aftermath of the global economic downturn and Kazakhstan's economic crisis of 2014, with the fall in oil prices and a major devaluation causing weaker domestic demand. More recently, the economy has begun to experience a rebound: Kazakhstan's annual GDP growth rate jumped from 1.1 percent in 2016 to 4.1 percent in 2017 and reached 4.5 percent in 2019.

FIGURE 1.1
Annual GDP growth, Kazakhstan, 2000–19

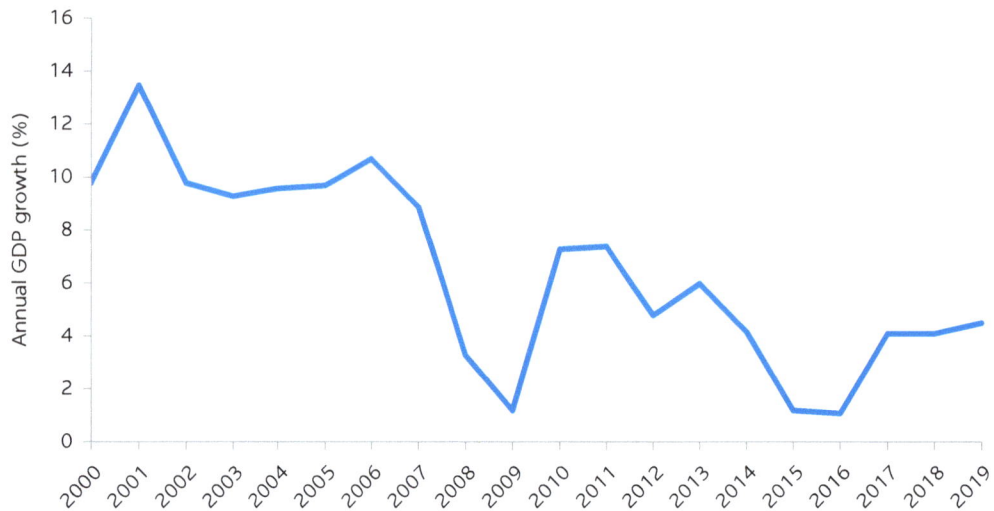

Source: World Bank, based on World Development Indicators data set.

Total factor productivity (TFP) has been an important driver of economic growth in Kazakhstan throughout this process. Productivity, defined as the technical efficiency with which firms transform inputs into production, is the ultimate driver of economic growth. As Krugman (1994, 11) famously claimed, "Productivity isn't everything, but, in the long run, it is almost everything. A country's ability to improve its standard of living over time depends almost entirely on its ability to raise its output per worker." In particular, growth in TFP—the efficiency with which multiple inputs, such as labor and capital, are transformed into production—is a major determinant of long-term economic growth (box 1.1). In Kazakhstan, TFP has been a crucial determinant of GDP growth over the past few decades, despite the major role that capital accumulation has played in most years. According to a recent Country Economic Memorandum (World Bank 2018), Kazakhstan experienced strong TFP growth during the early 2000s, with TFP contributing 6 percentage points, on average, to annual GDP growth. This period of strong productivity was followed by a decline in the 2008–09 period, a productivity resumption (at a much lower level) in 2010–13, and declining productivity in 2015–16, with the main driver of GDP growth being the capital base (figure 1.2).

Part of the slowdown in productivity growth—and thus GDP expansion—experienced in the 2010s reflects losses in the productivity engine within manufacturing and services. World Bank (2018) sheds light on the factors behind the TFP decline in the 2010s and shows that the global financial crisis had a pronounced effect on both the scale and the nature of productivity growth in Kazakhstan. Furthermore, it shows that the decrease in TFP growth since the 2010s has mirrored a decline in oil prices and reflects an expansion of jobs at the low-value end of the spectrum in manufacturing and services. Indeed, according to calculations presented in World Bank (2018), within-sector productivity improvements have been muted since 2010, with a collapse in productivity growth in the services sector and negative productivity growth in the

BOX 1.1

Determinants of economic growth: The importance of total factor productivity

Changes in real GDP in an economy are influenced by changes in available capital, labor, and technology. The "growth accounting equation" describes this relationship:

$$gY = \alpha K\, gK + \alpha L\, gL + gA,$$

where
gY is GDP growth,
gK is capital stock growth,
gL is labor force growth or population growth,
αK is capital's share of total income,
αL is labor's share of total income, and
gA is TFP (total factor productivity) growth.

TFP measures the efficiency with which countries transform factors of production and intermediate inputs into final outputs. Thus, changes in TFP reflect the development of production and process technologies in a country. Conceptually, TFP is measured as a residual, that is, that part of GDP growth that cannot be explained by the accumulation of factors of production (changes in capital stock and labor force). In simple terms, therefore, if labor and capital inputs remain unchanged between two periods, any changes in the output of a country would reflect changes in TFP.

For several decades, policy makers and researchers have emphasized the role of factor accumulation in fostering economic growth and development. However, more recently, cross-country empirical studies have shown that TFP growth accounts for more than half of income differences across the world and is a major determinant of long-term growth (for instance, Caselli 2005; Easterly and Levine 2001; Hsieh and Klenow 2010; Jones 2016). Figure B1.1.1 shows TFP plotted against GDP per worker for 118 countries in 2019. The two series are highly correlated, suggesting that TFP is a good predictor of GDP per capita.

FIGURE B1.1.1

Total factor productivity, by GDP per worker, 2019

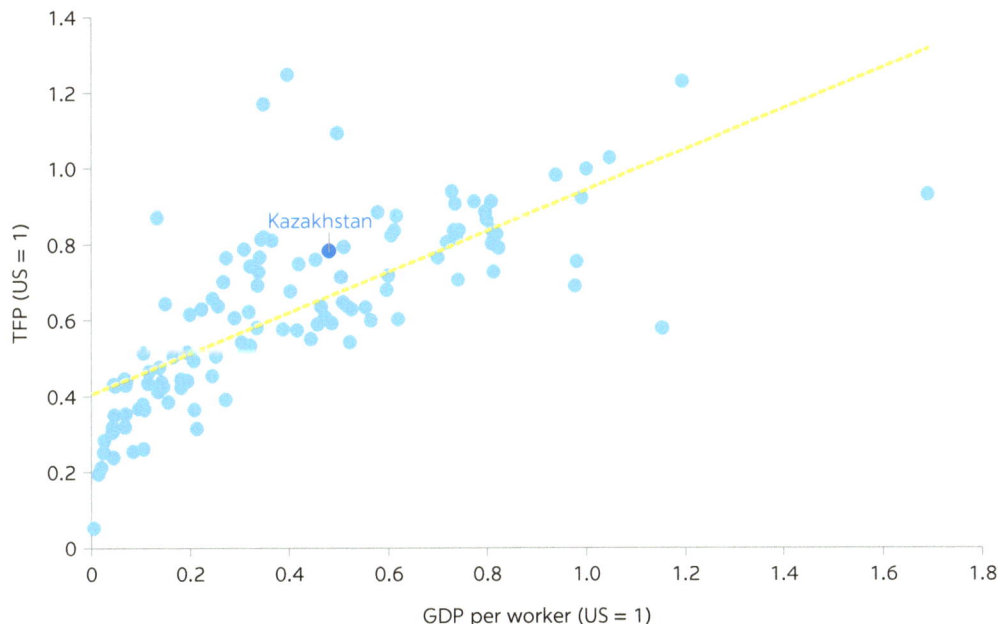

Source: Based on Penn World Tables Version 10.0 (Feenstra, Inklaar, and Timmer 2015).
Note: GDP = gross domestic product; TFP = total factor productivity.

FIGURE 1.2

Annual GDP growth decomposition, by factors of production, 2002–19

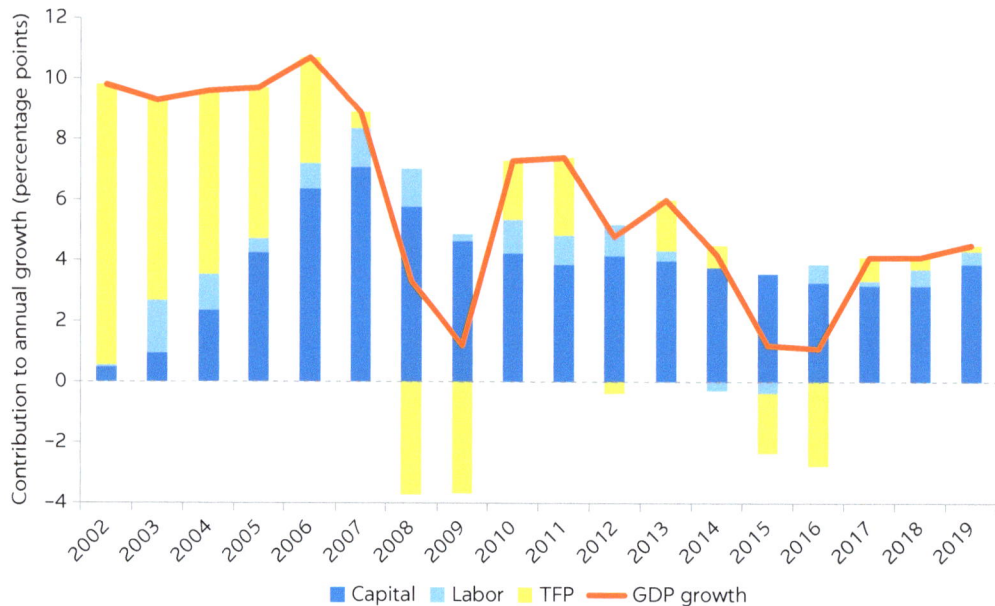

Source: World Bank, based on data from Kazakhstan Bureau of National Statistics and World Development Indicators data set.
Note: GDP = gross domestic product; TFP = total factor productivity.

manufacturing sector. For instance, labor has moved out of higher value added services (such as transport and communications) into lower-value services since 2010.

Low productivity growth outside the oil sector has also inhibited the spatial concentration and agglomeration effects that typically benefit countries at Kazakhstan's level of development. The spatial concentration of economic activities results from several factors, but an important one is the demand for labor in urban centers. Often reflecting a robust industrialization process, higher demand for labor in cities tends to increase urban-rural wage differentials, inducing the migration of workers to cities. Agglomeration is relevant not just for the agricultural sector but also for other sectors in rural areas, including services and small manufacturing. Economies of scale intrinsic to industrial sectors generate further agglomeration of economic activity and trigger a virtuous cycle of aggregate productivity gains. The low productivity growth of non-oil and urban sectors in Kazakhstan and a specialization in low value added services—two sides of the same coin—have inhibited such a virtuous cycle from fully developing.

THE QUEST TO RAISE PRODUCTIVITY AND THE NEED TO GO BEYOND AGGREGATE DATA

Kazakhstan needs to raise productivity in a sustained way to escape the "middle-income trap," so improving productivity growth outside the oil sector is paramount. Because Kazakhstan is an upper-middle-income economy with well-developed infrastructure and a relatively well-educated labor force, additional investments in physical capital will lead to diminishing returns on capital per worker and thus to limited growth of GDP per capita. In other words, because high rates of investment are no longer able to sustain substantial increases in income per capita, Kazakhstan must accelerate productivity growth to avoid decelerating growth in GDP per capita.[3] Accelerating productivity growth will require breaking the commodity cycle, which will only happen with an expanding productive and competitive private sector, diversified away from extractive industries.

The quest to boost productivity is not unique to Kazakhstan: in recent decades, productivity has stagnated in countries at all income levels. Dieppe (2020) shows that productivity has been slowing around the world. The 2007–09 global financial crisis triggered the steep fall-off in productivity among emerging market and developing economies. The causes included a wide set of factors that varied across countries. Among them were heightened policy uncertainty, lower growth in the advanced economies, adverse terms-of-trade shocks for commodity exporters, slowing foreign direct investment for commodity importers, and growing debt burdens. In advanced economies, the slowdown followed a trend that started in the late 1990s. Productivity stagnation in advanced economies has also been caused by a variety of factors. Among them are diminishing returns from technological progress, a pause in incorporating new digital technologies into production processes, and a broad-based weakness in investment driven by lack of demand.

Productivity growth is at the forefront of Kazakhstan's economic strategy. The Strategic Development Plan of the Republic of Kazakhstan until 2025 lists productivity growth as one of the critical drivers of economic transformation to lift Kazakhstan into the top 30 most developed countries by 2050.

Detecting the causes of low productivity growth and identifying policies to boost productivity performance, especially in the non-oil sector, require examining firm-level data. Identifying policies that can help the country promote productivity growth requires going beyond aggregate data. Aggregate trends in productivity (especially TFP) mask much heterogeneity (see box 1.2). For this reason, a macro-level analysis is not sufficient to identify the microeconomic dynamics contributing to the aggregate result, making it impossible to identify the underlying policy factors that drive the aggregate outcome. The client-funded Joint Economic Research Program Technical Assistance to Support Productivity Growth in Kazakhstan[4] explored firm-level data to deepen the understanding of the microeconomic dynamics and main drivers of aggregate productivity growth in the country and to identify a wide-ranging set of policy recommendations to boost aggregate productivity growth, especially outside the oil sector. The task encompassed three components: (1) "Setting the stage—Understanding micro-foundations of low-productivity growth," (2) "Government interventions and market contestability," and (3) "Innovation, entrepreneurship and SMEs [small and medium enterprises]." The current document summarizes the main findings of all deliverables produced under these three components and highlights the key policy recommendations, extracted from these deliverables, for boosting productivity growth in the country. Annex 1A describes the project's overall structure and lists the components and deliverables produced under this task.

BOX 1.2

Why is it essential to go beyond aggregate trends of productivity and use firm-level data?

To better understand obstacles to productivity growth and opportunities to overcome them, it is necessary to go beyond aggregate productivity trends and dive into firm-level analysis. Aggregate productivity numbers may be misleading. First, they might be affected by measurement problems, especially related to the emergence of information and communication technologies, that are difficult to capture in output statistics (Brynjolfsson, Rock, and Syverson 2017). Second, when measured as total factor productivity (TFP), aggregate productivity is estimated as the residual of an aggregate production function for the whole economy, ignoring technological differences across sectors within countries. Third, and probably most relevant for the current analysis, aggregate TFP figures mask heterogeneity in firm-level behavior. Firms differ in performance and other characteristics, even within very narrowly defined industries (Syverson 2004). These differences could persist either because of supply factors, such as management skills, research and development, or investment patterns (Bartelsman and Doms 2000), or because of demand factors related to product differentiation, customer-producer relationships, or geographical segmentation, among other causes.

Against this backdrop, it is crucial that firm-level data be used for a productivity diagnostic for several reasons. First, it complements aggregate analyses because it allows the evolution of economic variables (with or without cyclical frequencies) to be tracked (Haltiwanger 2007). Second, and more important for the policy perspective, firm-level data provide granular information for evidence-based policy making. Specifically, because there is much heterogeneity in firms' attributes and performance, the analysis of firm-level data allows the targeting and effectiveness of economic policies to be improved. In a context of heterogeneous performance and attributes across firms, designing policies that target the "average firm" may not have the desired impact.

ANNEX 1A: PROJECT DESCRIPTION: THE TECHNICAL ASSISTANCE TO SUPPORT PRODUCTIVITY GROWTH IN KAZAKHSTAN—MICRO DYNAMICS OF AGGREGATE PRODUCTIVITY GROWTH

The analytical work under the Joint Economic Research Program was conducted in fiscal year 2020/21 with the aim of setting the stage for deeper structural reforms (institutional capacity building, deregulation of services, and competition in product markets). The analytical work was split into three major components.

Component 1 ("Setting the stage—Understanding micro-foundations of low-productivity growth") focused on firm-level analysis and aimed to assess the micro-foundations of low productivity growth in Kazakhstan. It included three main deliverables: (1) decomposition of aggregate productivity, (2) analysis of agglomeration of economic activities, and (3) assessment of business environment and major bottlenecks for firm-level productivity growth.

Component 2 ("Government interventions and market contestability") aimed to deepen the understanding of low productivity growth in the nonhydrocarbon segments of the economy in Kazakhstan by focusing on the role of government interventions to strengthen market contestability. It included three main policy papers targeting the following objectives: (1) assessing the extent to which the current regulatory framework in Kazakhstan prevents competition at the economywide level, (2) assessing regulatory constraints to competition in key service (enabling) sectors, and (3) examining the current constraints (at both the strategic and institutional framework levels) that hamper the attraction of foreign direct investment into high-productivity sectors. All policy papers outline specific policy recommendations.

Component 3 ("Innovation, entrepreneurship, and SMEs") explored productivity determinants internal to the firm. It included two main policy papers: (1) a review of science, technology, and innovation policies and (2) a review of micro, small, and medium enterprise policies.

Component 4 envisages a report summarizing the main results and key policy recommendations. The structure of the work, including the deliverables, is summarized in figure 1A.1.

FIGURE 1A.1

Structure and deliverables of the "Technical Assistance to Support Productivity Growth in Kazakhstan" JERP task

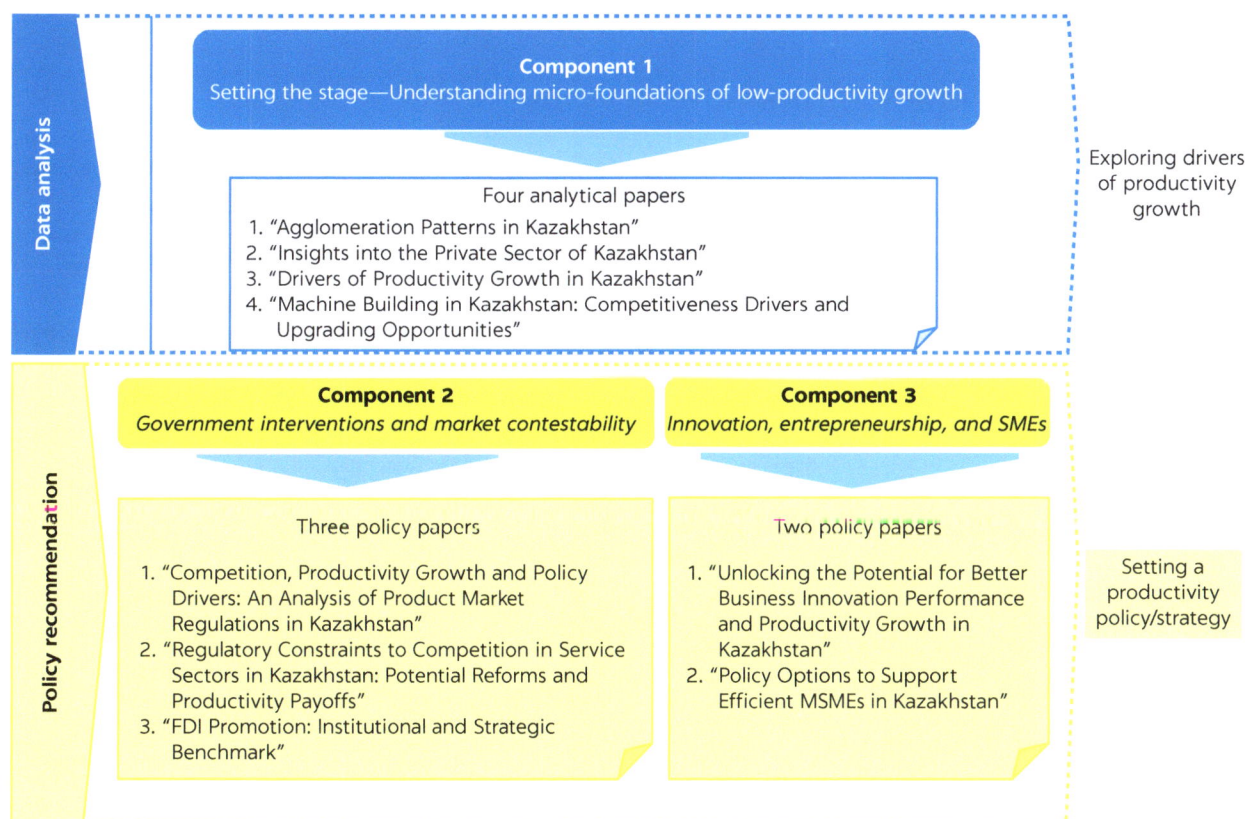

Source: World Bank.
Note: FDI = foreign direct investment; JERP = Joint Economic Research Program; MSMEs = micro, small, and medium enterprises; SMEs = small and medium enterprises.

NOTES

1. According to World Development Indicators data on "Poverty headcount ratio at $3.20 a day (2011 PPP) (% of population)" (https://data.worldbank.org/indicator/SI.POV.LMIC).
2. Calculation based on Penn World Tables Version 10.0.
3. As highlighted by World Bank (2018), maintaining the current investment in physical capital of about 25 percent of GDP per year would lead to only marginal increases in capital per worker and limited growth of GDP per capita. Without accelerating productivity growth, the economy would face ever-declining rates of growth in GDP per capita.
4. The "Technical Assistance to Support Productivity Growth in Kazakhstan—Micro Dynamics of Aggregate Productivity Growth in Kazakhstan" task under the Joint Economic Research Program (JERP) for FY 2020/21.

REFERENCES

Bartelsman, E. J., and M. Doms. 2000. "Understanding Productivity: Lessons from Longitudinal Microdata." *Journal of Economic Literature* 38 (3): 569–94.

Brynjolfsson, E., D. Rock, and C. Syverson. 2017. "Artificial Intelligence and the Modern Productivity Paradox: A Clash of Expectations and Statistics." In *Economics of Artificial Intelligence*, edited by Ajay Agrawal, Joshua Gans, and Avi Goldfarb, 23–59. Chicago: University of Chicago Press.

Caselli, F. 2005. "Accounting for Cross-Country Income Differences." In *Handbook of Economic Growth*, vol. 1, part A, edited by Philippe Aghion and Stephen Durlauf, 679–741. Amsterdam: Elsevier.

Dieppe, A., ed. 2020. *Global Productivity: Trends, Drivers, and Policies.* Washington, DC: World Bank.

Easterly, W., and R. Levine. 2001. "What Have We Learned from a Decade of Empirical Research on Growth? It's Not Factor Accumulation: Stylized Facts and Growth Models." *World Bank Economic Review* 15 (2): 177–219.

Feenstra, Robert C., Robert Inklaar, and Marcel P. Timmer. 2015. "The Next Generation of the Penn World Table." *American Economic Review* 105 (10): 3150–82. https://www.rug.nl/ggdc/productivity/pwt/related-research.

Haltiwanger, J. 2007. "Measuring and Analyzing Aggregate Fluctuations: The Importance of Building from Microeconomic Evidence." *Federal Reserve Bank of St. Louis Review* 79 (3): 55–78.

Hsieh, C.-T., and P. J. Klenow. 2010. "Development Accounting." *American Economic Journal: Macroeconomics* 2 (1): 207–23.

Jones, C. I. 2016. "The Facts of Economic Growth." *Handbook of Macroeconomics*, vol. 2, part A, edited by John B. Taylor and Harald Uhlig, 3–69. Amsterdam: Elsevier.

Krugman, P. R. 1994. *The Age of Diminished Expectations: U.S. Economic Policy in the 1990s.* Cambridge, MA: MIT Press.

Syverson, C. 2004. "Product Substitutability and Productivity Dispersion." *Review of Economics and Statistics* 86 (2): 534–50.

World Bank. 2018. "Kazakhstan: Reversing Productivity Stagnation. Country Economic Memorandum." World Bank Group, Washington, DC.

2 Micro Drivers of Productivity Growth

A FIRM-LEVEL ANALYSIS

INTRODUCTION

The empirical analysis drawing on firm-level data confirms a pattern of muted total factor productivity (TFP) growth in both manufacturing and services, with a modest expansion in the most recent years. Drawing from administrative firm-level data shared by the government of Kazakhstan, World Bank (Davies, Sakhonchik, and Correa 2021) analyzes productivity trends in Kazakhstan between 2009 and 2018. The analysis uses TFP as the key performance measure.[1] The results confirm a pattern of muted TFP growth, with moderate growth in the most recent years. After recovering from the global financial crisis of 2007–09, Kazakhstan's productivity growth started to slow in the early 2010s. Productivity growth declined even more with the economic crisis of 2014 following the fall in oil prices and a major devaluation, which weakened domestic demand and contributed to a gradual deterioration of potential output. The firm-level data confirm a decline in TFP between 2010 and 2015 in both manufacturing and services (figure 2.1).

FIGURE 2.1

Growth in total factor productivity, Kazakhstan, 2012–18

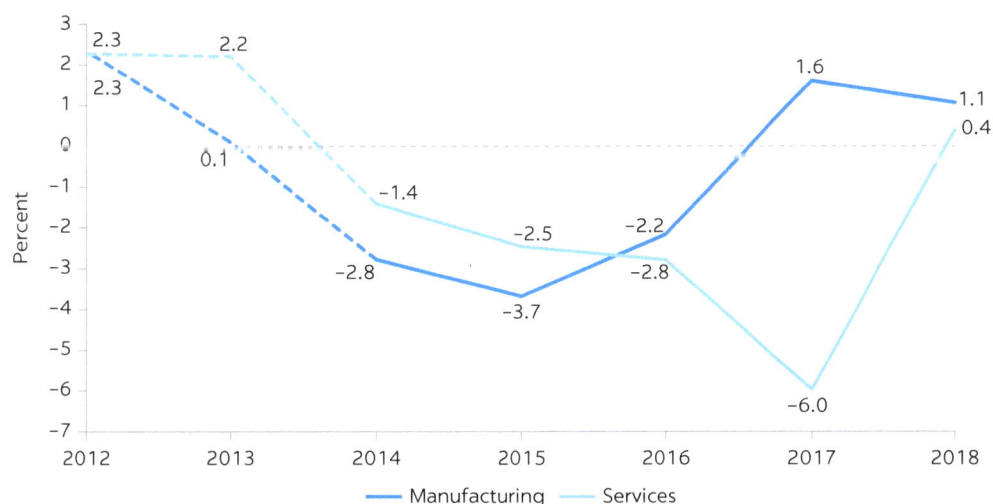

Source: Davies, Sakhonchik, and Correa 2021.
Note: The datapoints shown are three-year averages.

However, in more recent years, TFP growth has started to bounce back, albeit at a modest pace, possibly driven by the recovery in commodity prices. Between 2015 and 2018, TFP grew by 1.1 percent in the manufacturing sector and 0.4 percent in the services sector.

REGIONAL AND CROSS-INDUSTRY DISPARITIES IN PRODUCTIVITY

The regional and cross-industry disparities behind these recent numbers reflect the downshift in the productivity ladder and mirror the economy's heavy dependence on the extractives sector. The use of firm-level data allows the heterogeneity behind these numbers to be explored across both regions and industries. (Box 2.1 also discusses the heterogeneity at the level of the firm.)

As for regional disparities, World Bank (Davies, Sakhonchik, and Correa 2021) shows that the regions with the highest TFP growth in the 2015–18 period were Atyrau and Mangistau (17 percent and 10 percent, respectively) (panel a of figure 2.2); in both regions, mining activities play a key role in value added and employment. By contrast, Kostanay and Kyzylorda are among the regions that experienced the largest drops in productivity growth over the same period (declines of 10 percent and 8 percent, respectively). This result could be due to decreased labor productivity in the services sector (particularly accommodation and food services) in Kostanay and manufacturing in Kyzylorda (particularly in the wood and paper industry and computers and machinery).

When analyzing the results from a cross-industries perspective (panel b of figure 2.2), the activities with the largest productivity growth in the 2015–18 period were transport and storage (6 percent), mining (5 percent), and

FIGURE 2.2

Growth in total factor productivity, Kazakhstan, by region and sector, 2015–18

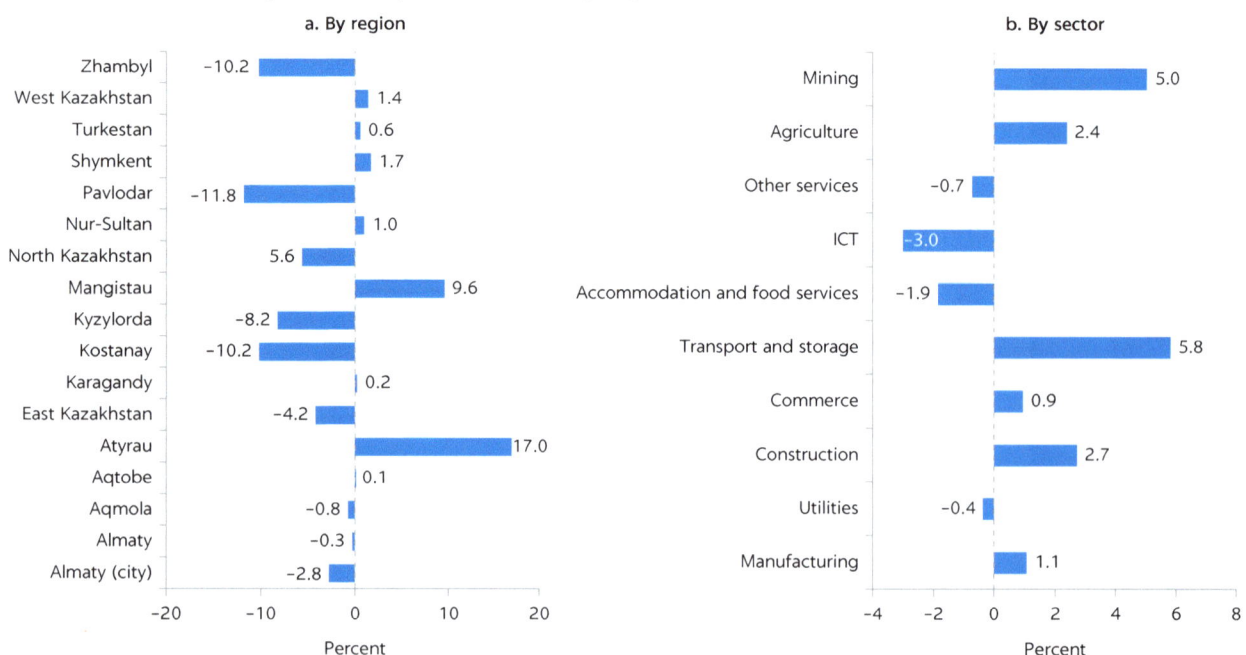

Source: Davies, Sakhonchik, and Correa 2021.
Note: ICT = information and communication technology.

BOX 2.1

Exploring the heterogeneity of productivity performance at the firm level in Kazakhstan

The analysis in World Bank (Davies, Sakhonchik, and Correa 2021) reveals substantial heterogeneity in firm performance in Kazakhstan. First, the data show that differences in sector, region, firm size and age, and capital explain only 40 percent of the observed differences in labor productivity, 7 percent of labor productivity growth, and 17 percent of total factor productivity (TFP) growth in the 2015–18 period (figure B2.1.1). In other words, performance in productivity growth and level are highly different even among firms in the same sector, in the same region, of the same size and age, and with similar levels of capital stock. Of the part that is explained, sector explains the largest portion (23 percent of the variation in labor productivity levels, 4 percent of the variation in labor productivity growth, and 16 percent

of the variation in TFP growth). Region explains about 5 percent of the variation in labor productivity and 8 percent of the variation in TFP while explaining very little of the variation seen in growth.

Second, there is also still much heterogeneity of firm productivity performance even within sectors, especially in the services sector. For example, in telecommunications in 2018, the productivity of a firm in the 90th percentile of TFP is three times as high as that of a firm in the 10th percentile (figure B2.1.2). High dispersion in productivity in a sector reflects distortions in the market that create a wedge in firms' performance. However, high-dispersion sectors are initial priorities for tailored policy interventions that could significantly benefit productivity growth by removing market distortions.

FIGURE B2.1.1

Share of productivity variation across firms explained by different factors, 2015–18

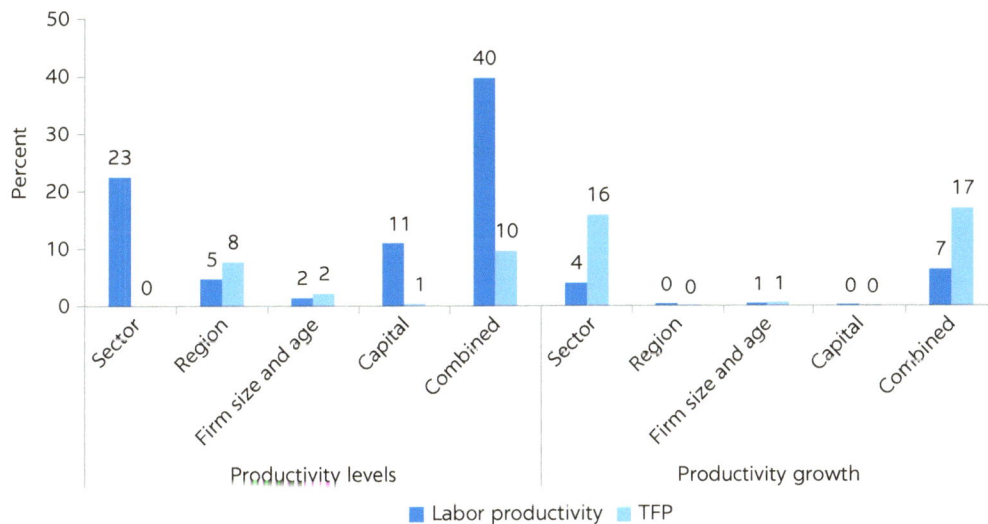

Source: Davies, Sakhonchik, and Correa 2021.
Note: The percentages correspond to the share of the variation in productivity explained by the factors included in the regression (R-squared). Sector is represented by a 5-digit industrial classifier (OKED) and firm size and age by size and age indicator variables (with age determined by the first appearance in the data set). The values for labor productivity, total factor productivity (TFP), and capital stock are in logs. Sector is excluded from the regressions on TFP because TFP was calculated by sector.

(Continued)

Box 2.1, *continued*

FIGURE B2.1.2

Total factor productivity dispersion, Kazakhstan, 2018

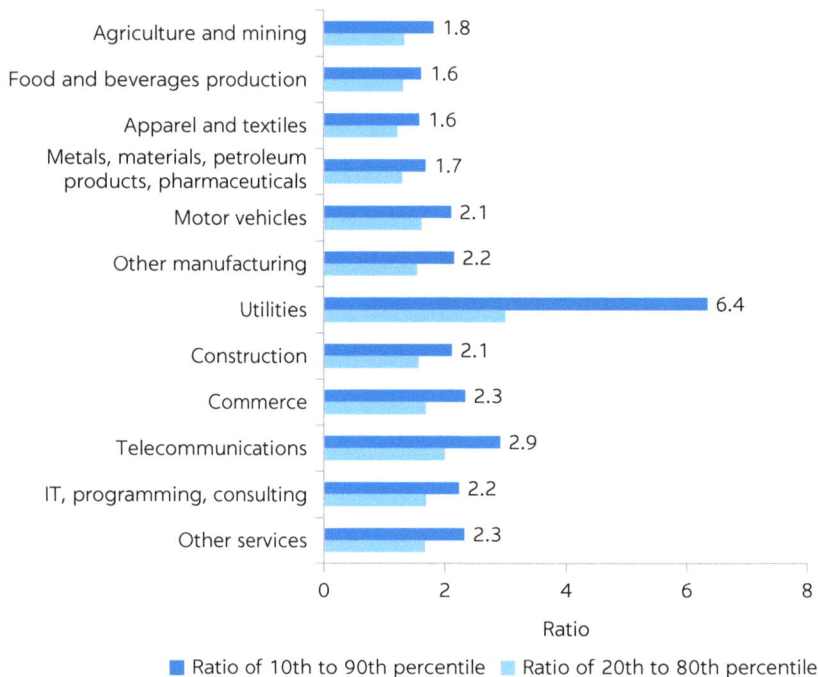

Source: Davies, Sakhonchik, and Correa 2021.
Note: The ratio is calculated by dividing total factor productivity (TFP) at the 90th or 80th percentile by TFP at the 10th or 20th percentile. For this calculation, TFP is in levels (not in logs). IT = information technology.

construction (3 percent). On the other end of the spectrum, the activities with the largest declines in TFP in the same period were information and communication technology (–3 percent), accommodation and food services (–2 percent), and other services (–1 percent). The group of high-productivity performers does not include high-value-added manufacturing (tradable) industries or skill-intensive services. Combined with the predominance of mining-dependent regions, this outcome reinforces the point that efficiency gains are not occurring in activities that could help diversify the economy. This downshift of the productivity engine reflects the supply-side characteristics of Kazakhstan's private sector, where it is considerably easier for businesses to enter and operate at the low end of the value added spectrum of activities.

THE ROOTS OF LOW PRODUCTIVITY: MUTED FIRM UPGRADING, POOR ALLOCATIVE EFFICIENCY, AND LIMITED BUSINESS DYNAMISM

Besides the heterogeneity across regions and industries, the micro-level analysis showed that Kazakhstan's modest productivity performance in the recent past, in both manufacturing and services, results from modest firm upgrading, poor allocative efficiency, and limited business dynamism. Aggregate productivity growth can be the result of three processes, which usually happen concurrently:

- *Improvement in firm capabilities.* Firms can become more productive when they innovate, adopt new technologies, and improve their organization and management practices (*within-firm* productivity growth).
- *Improvement in factor allocation.* Productivity can also improve if the factors of production move from lower- to high-productivity firms (*between-firm* productivity growth).
- *Productive entry and exit.* The entry of high-productivity firms and exit of low-productivity ones can also boost productivity (*entry and exit* productivity growth).

World Bank (Davies, Sakhonchik, and Correa 2021) applies the Melitz-Polanec methodology (Melitz and Polanec 2015) to decompose Kazakhstan's productivity growth over the 2011–18 period into these three elements. Results show that Kazakhstan experienced poor results across all three components in both the manufacturing and the services sectors. The between-firm effect, in particular, has been negative, on average. Meanwhile, the other two components have not been high enough to compensate and create a highly positive net effect. In fact, the net effect has been close to zero for both manufacturing and services. Overall, there was a low contribution of firm upgrading (within), poor allocative efficiency (between), and limited business dynamism (entry and exit) (figure 2.3).

Kazakhstan's weak performance becomes evident when compared with Poland, Serbia, and Slovenia, three countries where a similar micro-level productivity decomposition analysis was conducted. In all three, firm upgrading, promoting better allocation of production factors, and sponsoring more productive entry and exit played vital roles in achieving productivity growth. For example, in Poland in the early years after it made the transition to a market economy, 15 percent of productivity growth in manufacturing was due to gains

FIGURE 2.3

Melitz-Polanec decomposition of total factor productivity growth in manufacturing and services, Kazakhstan, 2011–18

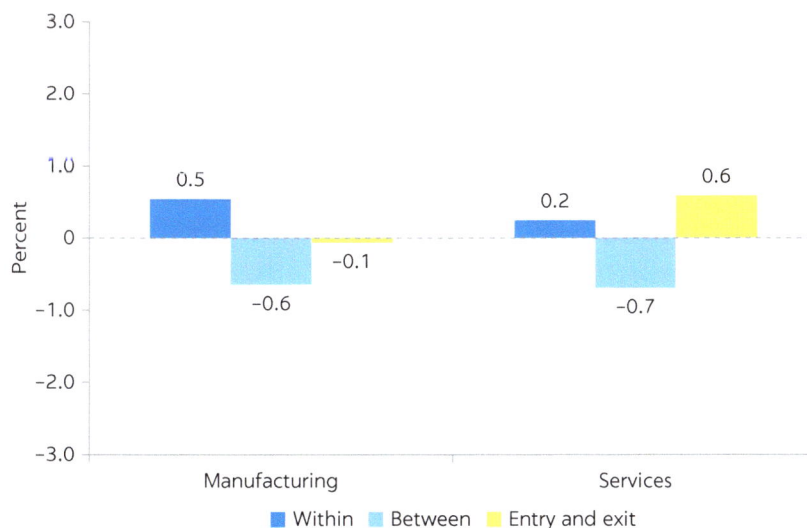

Source: Davies, Sakhonchik, and Correa 2021.

FIGURE 2.4

Melitz-Polanec decomposition of total factor productivity growth in manufacturing, Kazakhstan vs. selected peers, various years

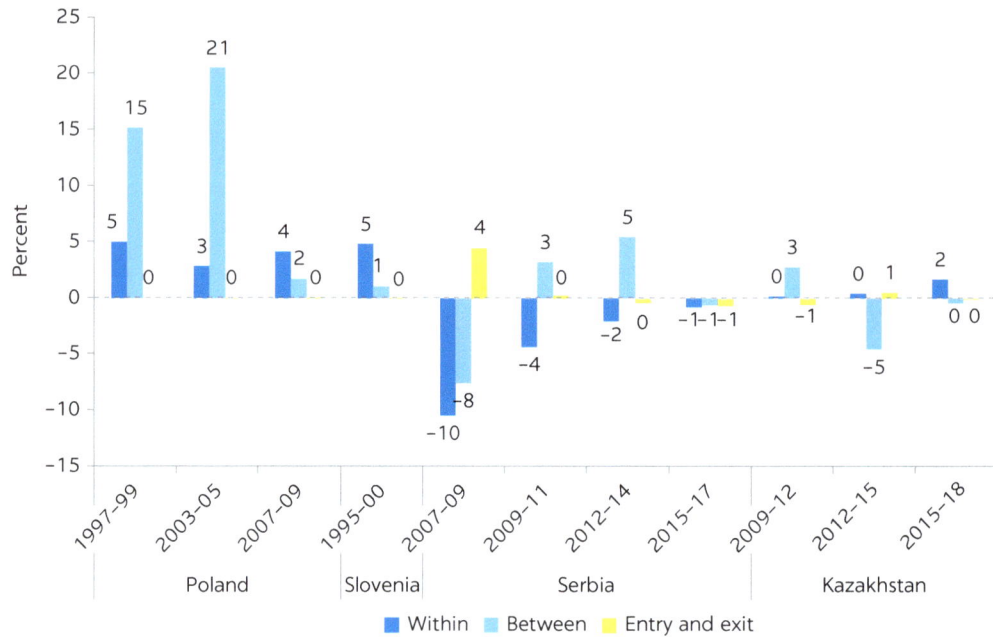

Source: Davies, Sakhonchik, and Correa 2021.

from allocative efficiency between firms (figure 2.4). The gains from a more efficient allocation of resources were even higher in the 2003–05 period at 21 percent. Similarly, in Serbia between 2009 and 2014, most productivity gains were achieved through better allocation of resources to more productive firms, allowing them to grow. However, this pattern reversed between 2014 and 2017, as economic transformation gave way to workaday market functioning.

PRIVATE SECTOR STAGNATION

A complementary analysis that zooms in on the performance of Kazakhstan's formal private sector offers additional insights: firms' entry is still insufficient, despite the reduction in costs to start a business. The entry of new firms into the formal sector is a standard proxy for entrepreneurship. Figure 2.5 displays the evolution of new firms' entry into the higher end of the formal sector in Kazakhstan during 2006–18; it is measured as the average annual number of new limited liability firms registered per 1,000 working-age people. As shown, the entry density rate has been experiencing an increasing trend, from 1.19 in 2006 to 2.0 in 2018. This might reflect the recent government efforts to reduce costs to start a new business. Indeed, according to Doing Business data, the cost to open a business shrank from 8.6 percent of income per capita in 2016/17 to 0.3 percent of income per capita in 2019/20. However, the same entry rates are still much lower than the regional averages in Europe and Central Asia. Most important, the average formal entry rate in Kazakhstan for the whole period is well below what would be predicted by the country's average income per capita in the same period (figure 2.6).

FIGURE 2.5

New firm entry density, Kazakhstan vs. Europe and Central Asia Region, 2006–18

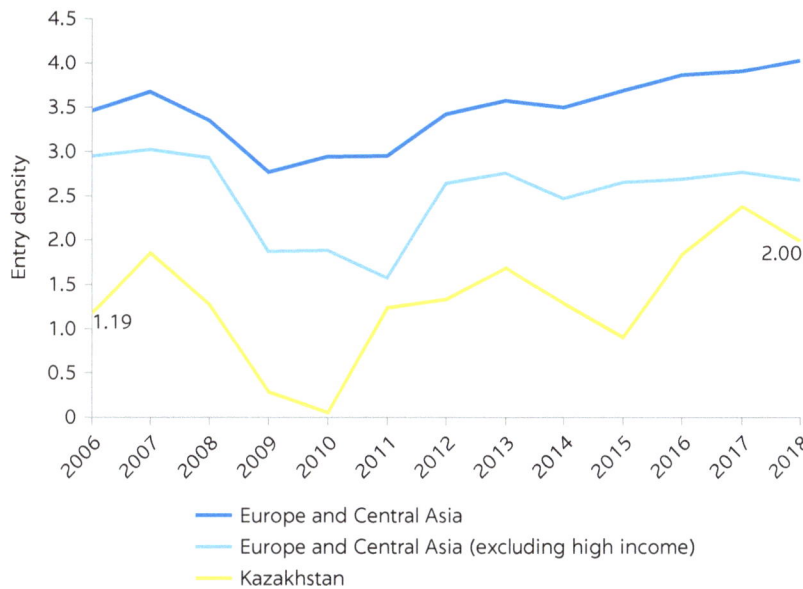

Source: Based on World Bank Entrepreneurship data set.
Note: New business entry density is defined as the number of newly registered formal, private limited liability firms per 1,000 working-age people (ages 15–64).

FIGURE 2.6

Average new business density, by average GDP per capita, 2006–18

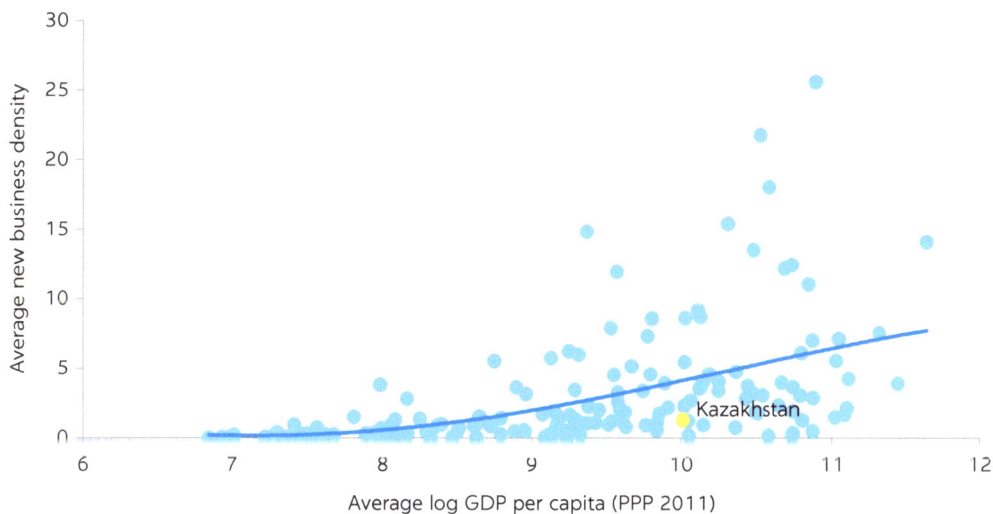

Source: Based on World Bank Entrepreneurship data set and World Bank World Development Indicators data set.
Note: New business entry density is defined as the number of newly registered formal, private limited liability firms per 1,000 working-age people (ages 15–64). GDP = gross domestic product; PPP = purchasing power parity.

Likewise, formal private firms do not grow as they age, reflecting a stagnant private sector. A crucial driver for economic development is the speed at which the average business grows over its life cycle (Eslava, Haltiwanger, and Pinzón 2019; Hsieh and Klenow 2014). Drawing on the latest round of World Bank Enterprise Survey data, World Bank (Karalashvili and Ueda 2021) compares the average age of (surviving) formal private firms to the average number of employees for Kazakhstan and two selected peer economies: Chile and the Russian Federation (panel a of figure 2.7). For all three countries, younger firms have smaller workforces than older firms. This result is consistent with patterns of selection and learning, given that firms tend to "learn" about their operations and productivity over time.[2] More interesting, however, is that cross-country differences in employment size widen as firms age. Kazakhstani formal private firms up to 10 years old employ, on average, only 14 workers, compared with 63 in Chilean peers. This gap grows wider (to almost 80 employees) for firms 20 or more years old. The gap between Russian and Kazakhstani formal firms also widens over time, though on a smaller scale: it jumps from a gap of 2 employees among firms up to 10 years old to 10 for firms 20 years old or older.[3] These results suggest that Kazakhstani private firms struggle to expand as they age. The breakdown of workforce-age profile by sector is rather revealing. Retail firms, where the growth profile is largest in Chile, remain mostly the same size in Kazakhstan across different age groups. Retail firms of any age in Kazakhstan employ about 14 workers, compared with 33, 76, and 110 across the three age groups in Chile. That is, in the retail sector, the disparity between firms in Kazakhstan and those in Chile grows as firms age (panel b of figure 2.7).

The fact that private sector firms are struggling to grow suggests that their productivity and performance are not being rewarded, reflecting a distortive

FIGURE 2.7
Average workforce in the formal private sector, by firm age group, Kazakhstan vs. selected peers

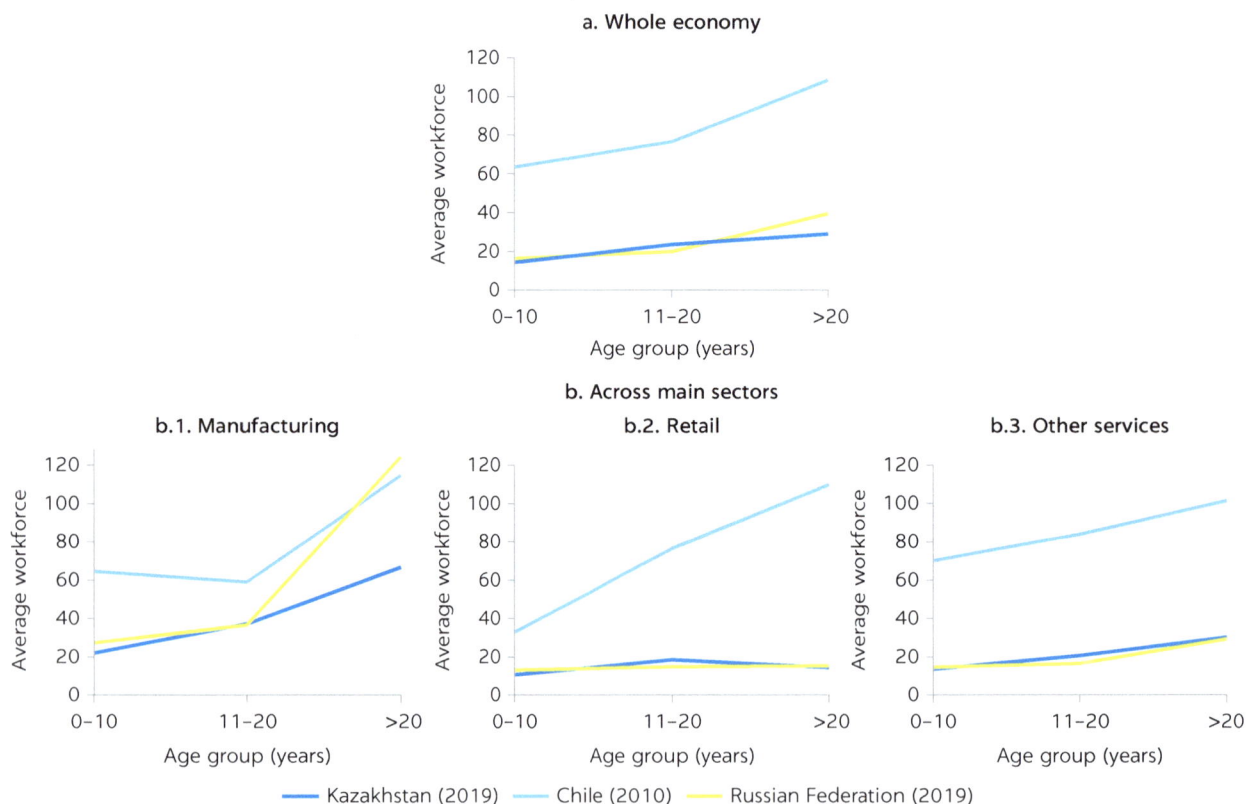

a. Whole economy

b. Across main sectors

b.1. Manufacturing

b.2. Retail

b.3. Other services

Kazakhstan (2019) — Chile (2010) — Russian Federation (2019)

Source: Karalashvili and Ueda 2021.
Note: The top decile (of firm size times World Bank Enterprise Survey sampling weights) was removed for each country to minimize volatility.

operating environment that interferes with allocating resources toward firms with higher productivity and growth potential. Conceptually, if firms "learn" about their productivity over time, one would expect that efficient firms would invest and expand, while less productive ones would stay small, shrink, or exit the market (Hopenhayn 1992; Jovanovic 1982). However, resource allocation does not occur naturally when the business environment is distorted such that it allows underperforming firms to survive or fails to provide incentives for efficient firms to grow. Hsieh and Klenow (2014) show that firm growth patterns diverge vastly across countries because of distortions that impede resource allocation toward firms with higher productivity and growth potential. Furthermore, the fact that the entry rate remains insufficient, despite the substantial reduction of administrative costs, suggests that additional distortions in the business environment might be playing a role in hampering private sector dynamism in Kazakhstan. While in specific circumstances, reducing the time and cost for a firm to enter a market or obtain a license can increase competition, this is often not the binding constraint for firm entry. In practice, the entry of new firms—and firm conduct afterward—are more influenced by regulatory barriers that determine the market's design, such as monopoly and exclusivity rights, price controls, and discriminatory or preferential access to inputs or finance. As discussed later in this report, several of these practices are still present in Kazakhstan, especially in sectors where state-owned enterprises operate.

TOWARD A COMPREHENSIVE PRODUCTIVITY POLICY

All these empirical results point to a common conclusion: Kazakhstan has room to leverage all three sources of productivity growth (improving firm capabilities, boosting factor allocation toward more productive firms, and enhancing productive entry and exit). A comprehensive productivity policy needs to encompass all three components of productivity growth (within, between, and entry and exit). The evidence provided by the Melitz-Polanec decomposition exercise shows that Kazakhstan must improve all these components, given that they have been low or negative, on average, in the 2011–18 period. Also the interdependencies among these components through endogenous and dynamic channels, as discussed below, must be borne in mind. The summative effect of the three components on TFP and their interdependencies mean that policy makers need to target all three.

Boosting productivity growth becomes even more critical in the context of COVID-19 (coronavirus) because the short-term effects from the pandemic can affect a country's long-term engines of productivity. The short-term effects of the pandemic on sales and employment are undoubtedly adverse in Kazakhstan. A recent analysis (World Bank 2021)—drawing on the follow-up survey to the standard World Bank Enterprise Survey—shows that sales from formal private firms in Kazakhstan have dropped substantially: average monthly sales in 2021 fell by 21 percent. The pandemic's impact on the workforce was also substantial: on average, 28 percent of formal private firms decreased the total number of hours worked per week relative to before the outbreak. However, it is still unclear how the crisis will affect the long-term trajectory of productivity growth in the country. For instance, the pandemic shock may negatively affect firm capabilities by irreversibly damaging intangible assets—such as buyer-supplier trust, lender-borrower relationships, and employee-firm relations—that would require new sunk-cost investments to re-create. Moreover, although the disruptions caused by the pandemic can push inefficient firms out of the market, it is unclear whether the firms that survive will be more productive. They may survive because they have other features not necessarily linked with efficiency, such as market power or rent-seeking ability. All these risks will require a rethinking of Kazakhstan's productivity policies. The ongoing short-term relief measures and the en masse vaccine rollout can help restore business confidence by beginning a reversion to the precrisis status quo. Still, long-term recovery requires that the root causes of Kazakhstan's low productivity growth be addressed to heat up the economy.

The climate change crisis compounds the challenges and calls for productivity policies that support a greener recovery fueled by creative destruction outside the oil sector. Solutions to twin crises of the COVID-19 pandemic and climate change need to be designed together. COVID-19 recovery programs and the strategies that will come from them are opportunities not only to regain lost economic ground but also to accelerate the green transition of the Kazakhstani economy. Kazakhstan is committed to reducing emissions by 15–25 percent by 2030, from the level of 1990. The country has also started the process of developing the Concept of Low Carbon Development until 2050.[4] To help micro, small, and medium enterprises tap into the opportunities that will emerge under this scenario, designing proactive policies to help them adapt to new environmental regulations and develop, adopt, and sell low-carbon and energy-efficient technologies and services will be crucial.

ANNEX 2A: METHODOLOGICAL APPROACH FOR PRODUCTIVITY ESTIMATION AND DECOMPOSITION USING ADMINISTRATIVE-LEVEL DATA

The analysis presented in World Bank (Davies, Sakhonchik, and Correa 2021) relied on administrative firm-level data covering 2009–18 that were collected for statistical purposes (see table 2A.1). These data cover business establishments across a range of sectors that include agriculture, mining, manufacturing, construction, commerce (wholesale and retail trade), transport, accommodation and food service activities, information and communication technology, and other services (based on the International Standard Industrial Classification 2-digit industrial classification). The most prominent sector is "other services" (for example, personal services, recreation services), with 34 percent of firms accounting for 21 percent of employment. Next is the commerce sector, with 15 percent of firms accounting for 12 percent of employment. In the manufacturing sector, 9 percent of firms account for 18 percent of employment.

The data are collected at the level of the business establishment (local production unit). The largest shares of establishments are in the main business cities of Almaty (15 percent) and Nur-Sultan (10 percent), representing 19 percent and 9 percent of employment, respectively. The share of establishments covered in the rest of the country varies from as high as 7 percent in East Kazakhstan and 6 percent in Aqmola to as low as 4 percent in Aqtobe, Kyzylorda, Mangistau, North and West Kazakhstan, and Zhambyl, and 3 percent in the city of Shymkent.

Large establishments account for 2 percent of all firms in the data set (2018) and 47 percent of total employment. Small and medium enterprises represent one-fourth of all establishments covered by the data set, with

TABLE 2A.1 Sectoral and regional coverage of the establishment-level administrative data

| REGION OR CITY | NUMBER OF ESTABLISHMENTS WITH EMPLOYMENT, 2018 | | | |
	MANUFACTURING	SERVICES	OTHER AND PRIMARY	TOTAL
Almaty	785	7,057	293	8,135
Almaty Region	467	2,722	628	3,817
Aqmola Region	348	2,244	938	3,530
Aqtobe Region	197	1,660	320	2,177
Atyrau Region	108	2,483	131	2,722
East Kazakhstan	410	2,930	484	3,824
Karagandy Region	554	3,837	439	4,830
Kostanay Region	259	1,784	453	2,496
Kyzylorda Region	135	1,771	278	2,184
Mangistau Region	152	1,813	216	2,181
North Kazakhstan	193	1,286	679	2,158
Nur-Sultan	346	5,061	214	5,621
Pavlodar Region	318	2,064	247	2,629
Shymkent	165	1,105	142	1,412
Turkestan Region	237	1,693	1,075	3,005
West Kazakhstan	169	1,878	197	2,244
Zhambyl Region	217	1,577	254	2,048
All cities and regions	5,093	43,202	7,125	55,420

Source: Davies, Sakhonchik, and Correa 2021.
Note: The figures only include establishments with at least one employee active in 2018. "Other and primary" includes agriculture, mining, and other primary activities. Services includes construction and utilities. For 407 establishments, no region or city was reported.

47 percent of total employment. The data do not contain information on informal (unregistered) establishments or informally employed workers.

The data provide information on employment, payroll, wages, material costs, volume of production and sales, capital stock, financial liabilities, and total current and fixed assets, among others. However, information on ownership status, imports, exports, and the founding date of the business is missing. For the purposes of the analysis, the first appearance in the data set serves as a proxy for age.

Drawing from this data set, productivity was estimated as TFP, which measures the efficiency of how the economy transforms multiple factors of production (capital, labor, and so on) to production output. Specifically, TFP was estimated by calculating the share of output that is not explained by the quantity of factors of production used in production (the "residual"). In a production function $Y=A\ K\alpha L\beta$, in which Y is output, K is the amount of capital, and L the amount of labor, TFP is equal to A. Because no firm-level price indexes were available in the data set, the analysis relied on revenue-based measures of total factor productivity (TFPR), with prices deflated at the industry level using the production price index. It is worth acknowledging that because TFPR measures output in value terms, it incorporates both physical output and the prices charged, which leads to a potential upward bias in productivity estimates for those firms with market power.

BOX 2A.1

Dynamic Olley-Pakes decomposition (Melitz and Polanec 2015)

The dynamic Olley-Pakes decomposition proposed by Melitz and Polanec (2015) allows for the attribution of productivity growth to these factors: within-firm productivity growth, between-firm growth, and dynamic productivity growth. The productivity decomposition proposed by Melitz and Polanec (2015) allows for disentangling productivity, based on the following equation:

$$\Delta\Phi = \Delta\bar{\phi}_S + \Delta cov_S + s_{E2}(\Phi_{E2} - \Phi_{S2}) + s_{X1}(\Phi_{S1} - \Phi_{X1}).$$

In the equation, $\Delta\Phi$ is the (weighted) growth in revenue total factor productivity (TFPR), $\Delta\bar{\phi}_S$ is the unweighted growth in TFPR for surviving firms (the change in the simple average of TFPR, corresponding to the "within" component);

$\Delta cov_S = \Delta[\sum_i (s_{it} - \bar{s}_i)(\phi_{it} - \bar{\phi}_t)]$ is the change in covariance of market share and productivity (corresponding to the "between" component); the third term represents the productivity difference between entrants and surviving firms (the "entry" component); and the fourth term represents the difference in productivity between surviving firms and exiting firms (the "exit" component).

The "between" firm growth component can be further decomposed to separate the effect describing within-industry reallocations (inter-industry) and a term describing shifts between different industries within a sector (intra-industry). In this analysis, market share is calculated by the value added contributed by the firm, following the practice of Melitz and Polanec (2015).

Once TFPR was estimated for each firm, the dynamic Olley-Pakes decomposition—as developed by Melitz and Polanec (2015)—was applied to attribute productivity growth to three elements: within-firm productivity growth, between-firm growth, and dynamic productivity growth.

Box 2A.1 explains the mechanics behind the Melitz and Polanec (2015) methodology.

NOTES

1. See annex 2A for a description of the data set used in this analysis and the methodology applied to estimate TFP.
2. According to several models of business dynamics, firms "learn" about their productivity over time, so efficient firms invest and expand, while less productive ones stay small, shrink, or exit the marketplace. See, for instance, Jovanovic (1982).
3. Russian formal private firms up to 10 years old employ on average 16 workers (compared with 14 among Kazakhstani firms); for firms 20 years or more old, Russian firms employ on average 39 workers (compared with 29 among firms in Kazakhstan).
4. At the UN Climate Ambition Summit in December 2020, Kazakhstan's President Kassym-Jomart Tokayev set a new goal for Kazakhstan—to achieve carbon neutrality by 2050. Doing so will require development of long-term, systemic measures to decarbonize the national economy.

REFERENCES

Davies, E., A. Sakhonchik, and P. Correa. 2021. "Drivers of Productivity Growth in Kazakhstan." World Bank, Washington, DC.

Eslava, M., J. Haltiwanger, and A. Pinzón. 2019. "Job Creation in Colombia vs the US: "Up or Out Dynamics" Meets "The Life Cycle of Plants." Working Paper 25550, National Bureau of Economic Research, Cambridge, MA.

Hopenhayn, H. 1992. "Entry, Exit, and Firm Dynamics in Long Run Equilibrium." *Econometrica* 60 (5): 1127–50.

Hsieh, C.-T., and P. J. Klenow. 2014. "The Life Cycle of Plants in India and Mexico." *Quarterly Journal of Economics* 29 (3): 1035–84.

Jovanovic, B. 1982. "Selection and the Evolution of Industry." *Econometrica* 50 (3): 649–70.

Karalashvili, N., and K. Ueda. 2021. "Insights into the Private Sector of Kazakhstan." World Bank, Washington, DC.

Melitz, M., and S. Polanec. 2015. "Dynamic Olley-Pakes Productivity Decomposition with Entry and Exit." *RAND Journal of Economics* 46 (2): 362–75.

World Bank. 2021. "Enterprise Surveys Follow-Up on COVID-19: Kazakhstan." World Bank Group, Washington, DC.

3 Policy Diagnosis and Recommendations

INTRODUCTION

Policies to boost productivity growth can be clustered into measures that affect the operating environment of firms and those that affect firm upgrading. The ability of firms to grow and become more productive stems from the combination of multiple policies (figure 3.1).[1] A solid productivity policy mix should target two goals simultaneously to affect all three components of productivity. One is *removing distortions in the operating environment of firms* so productive resources are allocated toward firms with higher productivity and growth potential while high-productivity firms enter and low-productivity ones exit. Achieving this goal would positively affect the "between" and "entry and exit"

FIGURE 3.1
Drivers of productivity growth

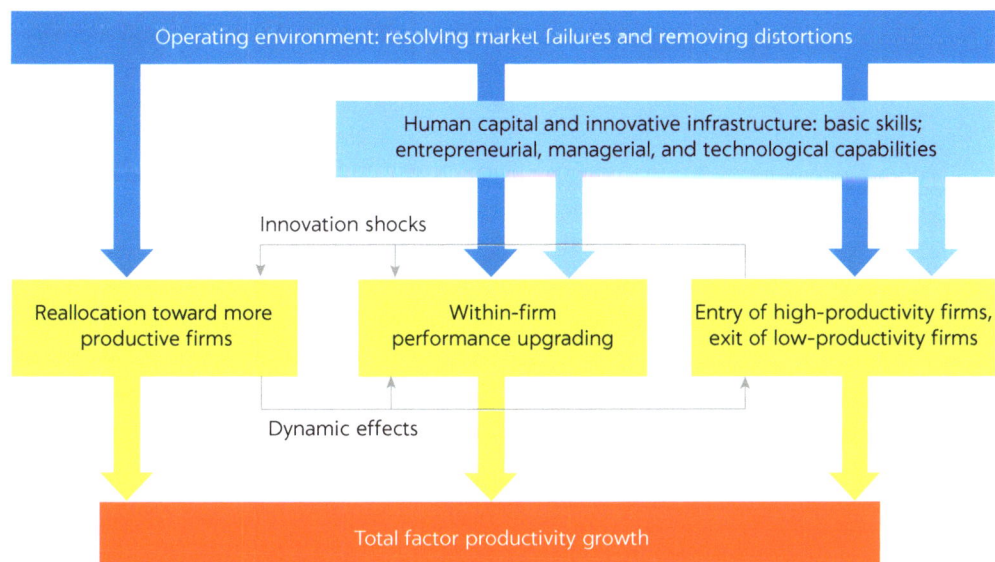

Source: Cusolito and Maloney 2018.

components of productivity growth. The other goal is *facilitating the upgrading of firms' capabilities* so that firms can identify new opportunities in the market, take risks to develop and adopt new technologies, and expand their activities. Achieving this goal would bring positive dividends to the "within" component of productivity growth.

Against this backdrop, the analysis for Kazakhstan reveals four main (interrelated) issues to be addressed, as discussed in the sections that follow.

REMOVING COMPETITION DISTORTIONS IN THE PRODUCT MARKETS TO ALLOW MORE PRODUCTIVE FIRMS TO GROW FASTER

Competition is a crucial ingredient for productivity growth. Competition[2] boosts aggregate productivity through all three components. It promotes allocative efficiency by allowing more efficient firms to gain market share or obtain more productive inputs at the expense of less efficient firms (the "between-firm" component). It also boosts market selection by facilitating the entry of more productive firms and encouraging the exit of less productive ones (the "selection" or "entry and exit" component). Finally, competition generates dynamic effects by encouraging incumbent firms to upgrade their internal capabilities, increasing productive efficiency at the firm level (the "within-firm" component).

In turn, government interventions can influence the competitive pressure in the domestic market—and thereby affect the productivity performance of domestic firms—in various ways. Governments can influence competition directly and indirectly. As direct market players, they can buy inputs (through public procurement) and sell products and services (through state-owned enterprises [SOEs]). Governments can also influence market outcomes indirectly by setting rules and creating institutions that shape market dynamics. Regulation, subsidies, taxation, and competition and antitrust rules can influence competition by affecting the possibility of market entry or exit,[3] the ability of firms to compete in the market,[4] and the ability of consumers to shop around between firms and exercise consumer choice (Office of Fair Trading 2009). In this context, governments can level the playing field and encourage the smooth functioning of markets by implementing a comprehensive competition policy framework. Such a framework rests on three key pillars: (1) fostering procompetition regulations and government interventions in markets, (2) promoting competitive neutrality and nondistortive public aid, and (3) enabling effective competition law and antitrust enforcement (Kitzmueller and Licetti 2012).

By improving Kazakhstan's competition policy framework, the government has taken important steps to implement procompetition reforms and level the playing field. Kazakhstan has made some progress on its institutional framework for enforcing competition policy and law. In January 2015, Kazakhstan became a member of the Eurasian Economic Union, requiring the government to align its competition law with the union's standards. In May 2015, Kazakhstan adopted an action plan for economic development, "100 concrete steps," which envisaged several institutional reforms, including reforms of the antitrust authorities and corresponding legislation to align them with standards and best practices in the Organisation for Economic

Co-operation and Development (OECD). In January 2016, the Entrepreneurial Code—which incorporates and supersedes the 2008 law on Competition and Natural Monopolies and Regulated Markets—entered into force and introduced some new tools of antitrust response as well as tools to combat cartels, such as "dawn raids."[5] On September 8, 2020, the president issued Decree No. 407 creating the Agency for Protection and Development of Competition of the Republic of Kazakhstan. On October 5, 2020, Presidential Decree No. 428 laid out the foundational charter of this competition agency. It is responsible for enforcing Kazakhstan's laws and regulations related to the protection and development of competition, including merger regulations and antitrust enforcement (as set forth in Part 4 of the Entrepreneurial Code of the Republic of Kazakhstan of October 29, 2015). It is directly accountable to the president and replaces the Committee for the Protection and Development of Competition, which was subordinate to and legally dependent on the Ministry of National Economy (MNE).

Because competition authorities require a substantial degree of independence to conduct their activities in a nonpartisan, competent, and effective manner, establishing the new competition agency outside the government ministries is a major achievement in limiting the scope for political intervention in its activities. The effective independence of this new competition agency remains to be seen in practice. It will depend on critical features of the agency's structure: its budget independence, its governance structure, and its relationship to other state bodies with concurrent powers to implement competition policy in Kazakhstan (such as the sector regulators). In any case, at least on paper, the creation of this new competition agency is an improvement.

Although all these recent measures are relevant and are important milestones, there is still space for improvement. In particular, Kazakhstan's regulatory framework for product markets is considerably more restrictive to competition than those in key peer countries. World Bank (Borja, Pop, and Sakhonchik 2021) draws on the 2018 OECD Product Market Regulation (PMR) database to assess the extent to which public policies promote or inhibit market forces in Kazakhstan. The aggregate economywide PMR indicator sheds light on specific restrictions of the regulatory framework (as they appear as a matter of record) via two main pillars: (1) distortions induced by state involvement and (2) barriers that can hamper entry of domestic and foreign firms and products into the market. The analysis finds that PMR in Kazakhstan (as a matter of record) is considerably more restrictive to competition than the regulatory frameworks in Eastern European OECD member countries and the OECD average (figure 0.2).[6]

Most of the restrictions come from distortions induced by state involvement in the economy. These distortions result from a combination of several factors. First and foremost is the direct state involvement through SOEs in a wide range of sectors, including those in which competition from the private sector is feasible. For instance, data show that of 29 broad sectors covered by the 2018 PMR database, the government of Kazakhstan controls SOEs in at least 20. This level of state ownership significantly exceeds the average number of sectors with at least one SOE in OECD economies (13) and non-OECD economies (14.5). As highlighted in World Bank (Borja, Pop, and Sakhonchik 2021), although state involvement may be necessary in some network sectors with high capital outlays, Kazakhstani SOEs participate in product markets where there is a less clear economic rationale for state

FIGURE 3.2

Economywide PMR scores and composition, Kazakhstan and comparator countries, 2018

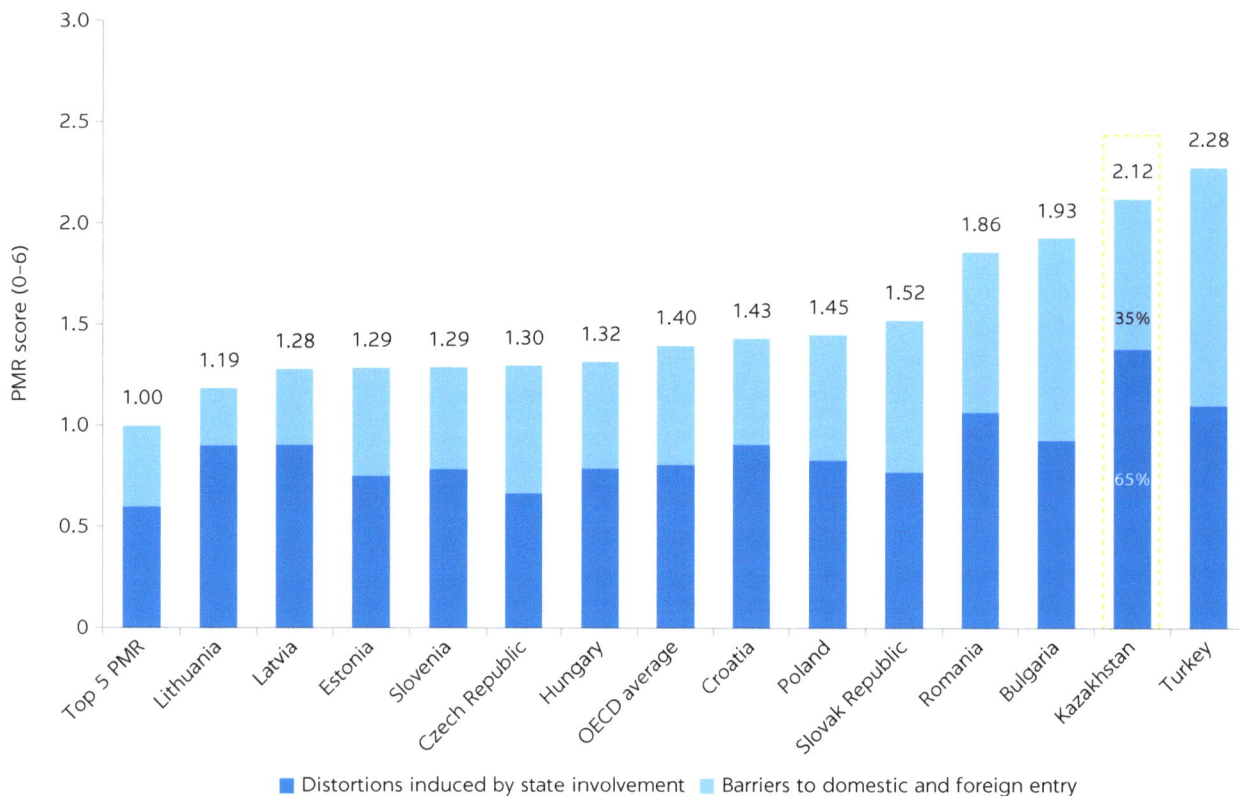

■ Distortions induced by state involvement ■ Barriers to domestic and foreign entry

Source: Borja, Pop, and Sakhonchik 2021.
Note: The Product Market Regulation (PMR) score is an index from 0 (least restrictive) to 6 (most restrictive). The top 5 performers in the overall PMR economywide indicator are the United Kingdom, Denmark, Spain, Germany, and the Netherlands. The Organisation for Economic Co-operation and Development (OECD) average includes 36 countries.

intervention. As an example, Kazakhstani SOEs are active in sectors such as gas supply, retail e-communication services, air transport, manufacturing, accommodation, and banking services. Second, SOEs compete on uneven (nonneutral) terms with the private sector because of gaps in the regulatory framework and its implementation. For instance, the state provides budget support and other financial advantages to SOEs—such as state guarantees and subsidized loans—giving SOEs an advantage compared with private sector operators (see box 3.1 for further discussion and more examples). Third, restrictive public procurement policies play a role. The analysis presented in World Bank (Borja, Pop, and Sakhonchik 2021) shows that competition remains limited in public procurement. For instance, in 2019, single-source procurement accounted for 49 percent of procurement value by public entities and about 80 percent of procurement value by SOEs.[7] Fourth, the continued use of price control mechanisms may also create market distortions and affect strategic decisions in workably competitive markets. According to the 2018 PMR database, of the 46 economies covered, governments in 7 economies, including Kazakhstan, still control retail prices in workably competitive markets.[8] For instance, the government of Kazakhstan controls the margins of 19 staple food products.[9]

Barriers to competition in network sectors are also sizable. The level of regulatory restrictiveness to competition in network sectors is high in

Kazakhstan compared with the OECD average (figure 3.3).[10] The economic literature has demonstrated that regulatory constraints on competition in services markets inhibit not only the use of services as inputs in the production process of downstream sectors (that is, manufacturing) but also the countries' potential to capitalize on higher productivity growth (Arnold, Javorcik, and Mattoo 2011; Arnold et al. 2015; Barone and Cingano 2011). The analysis in World Bank (Van der Marel, Iootty, and Bizhan 2021) reveals that the rate of services input usage by the manufacturing sector is low in Kazakhstan when compared with most of its upper-middle-income peers.[11] This low rate of input services use means that the country still has much untapped potential for employing input services by firms and industries to generate higher productivity, thereby creating higher income. Reaping these benefits from services requires that markets in services be competitive. The same World Bank (Van der Marel, Iootty, and Bizhan 2021) analysis sheds light on two specific services sectors—transport logistics and

---

BOX 3.1

Key highlights from a competitive neutrality analysis in Kazakhstan

Although direct state involvement in the markets is not in itself a problem from a market outcome point of view, ensuring competitively neutral policies for public and private operators is essential. It is important to ensure that the participation of the government in the economy remains subsidiary to that of the private sector, that is, that the state provides only those goods and services that the private sector cannot provide itself. Embedding competition principles in policy making may minimize potential distortions from direct state intervention through state-owned enterprises (SOEs), including through state aid. In this respect, it is essential to review (1) whether the SOE occupies a significant position in the market, (2) whether regulations or policies protect SOEs from market competition, and (3) whether the private sector could provide those services or goods in a more efficient manner.

A preliminary assessment of competitive neutrality gaps in Kazakhstan (Borja, Pop, and Sakhonchik 2021) reveals that there are several areas in which policies could be reformed to level the playing field between private and public operators. Key regulatory shortcomings identified by this preliminary exercise include the following:

- The state provides budget support and other financial advantages—such as state guarantees or subsidized loans—to SOEs, which places SOEs at an advantageous position compared with private sector operators. For instance, Samruk-Kazyna (SK) received US$14 billion from the state to finance its operations during 2008–16. SK also has special privileges not granted to other companies, such as the preemptive right to buy strategic facilities and bankrupt assets and exclusion from some government procurement procedures.

- There is no legal requirement or systematic separation between commercial and noncommercial activities of the SOEs, which allows them to use the resources from noncommercial activities to cross subsidize commercial activities where they face competition from private operators.

- Finally, there is no express requirement for SOEs to achieve a commercial rate of return, which increases the risk of supporting inefficient firms. For instance, the three largest SOE funds (SK, Baiterek, and KazAgro) show decreasing returns on equity and productivity over time, despite having received capital injections from the government.

Figure B3.1.1 summarizes firm-level and cross-cutting policies that are needed to level the playing field in the market between public and private operators in Kazakhstan.

(Continued)

Box 3.1, *continued*

FIGURE B3.1.1

Competitive neutrality gap analysis

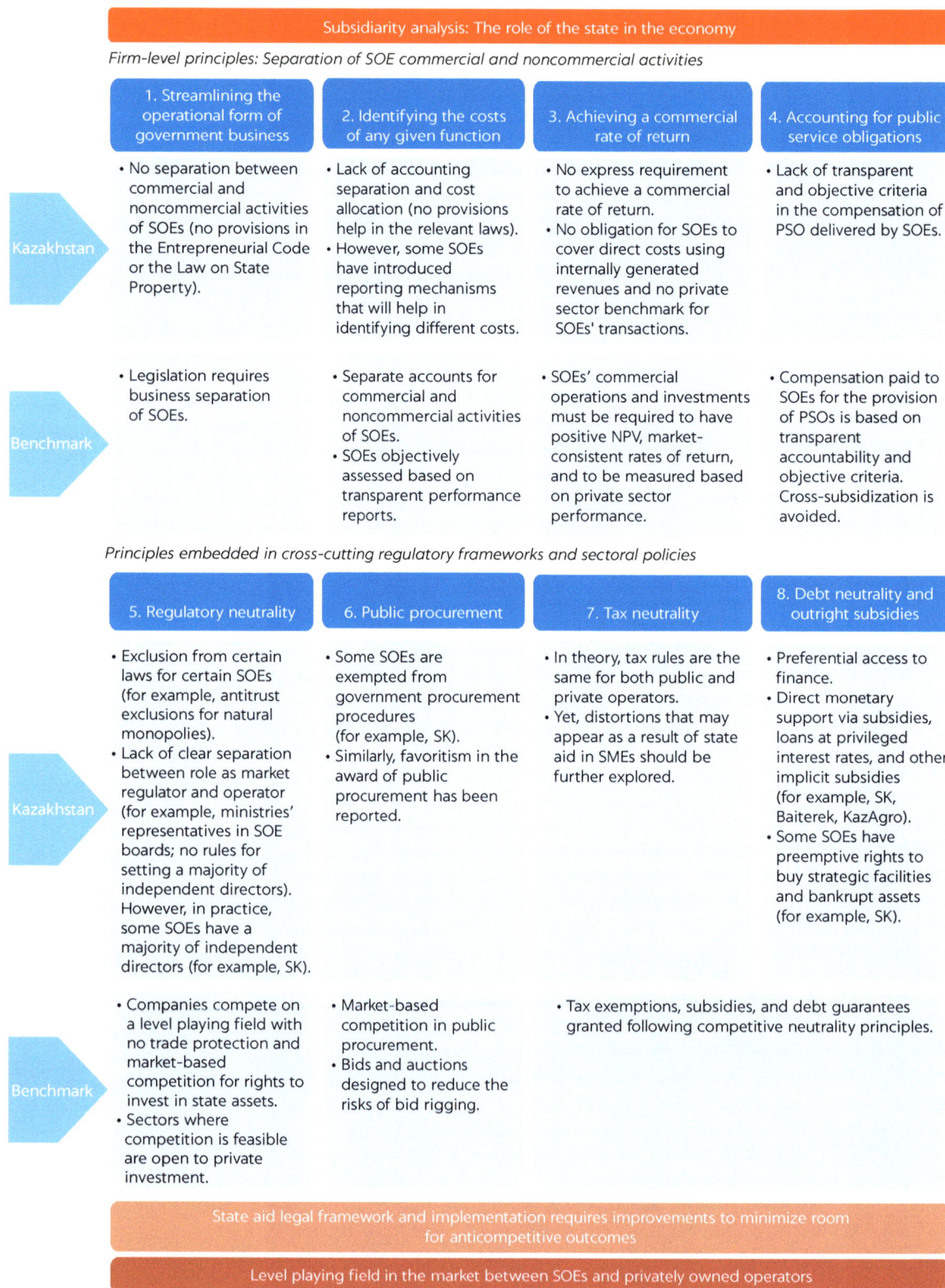

Subsidiarity analysis: The role of the state in the economy			

Firm-level principles: Separation of SOE commercial and noncommercial activities

	1. Streamlining the operational form of government business	2. Identifying the costs of any given function	3. Achieving a commercial rate of return	4. Accounting for public service obligations
Kazakhstan	• No separation between commercial and noncommercial activities of SOEs (no provisions in the Entrepreneurial Code or the Law on State Property).	• Lack of accounting separation and cost allocation (no provisions help in the relevant laws). • However, some SOEs have introduced reporting mechanisms that will help in identifying different costs.	• No express requirement to achieve a commercial rate of return. • No obligation for SOEs to cover direct costs using internally generated revenues and no private sector benchmark for SOEs' transactions.	• Lack of transparent and objective criteria in the compensation of PSO delivered by SOEs.
Benchmark	• Legislation requires business separation of SOEs.	• Separate accounts for commercial and noncommercial activities of SOEs. • SOEs objectively assessed based on transparent performance reports.	• SOEs' commercial operations and investments must be required to have positive NPV, market-consistent rates of return, and to be measured based on private sector performance.	• Compensation paid to SOEs for the provision of PSOs is based on transparent accountability and objective criteria. Cross-subsidization is avoided.

Principles embedded in cross-cutting regulatory frameworks and sectoral policies

	5. Regulatory neutrality	6. Public procurement	7. Tax neutrality	8. Debt neutrality and outright subsidies
Kazakhstan	• Exclusion from certain laws for certain SOEs (for example, antitrust exclusions for natural monopolies). • Lack of clear separation between role as market regulator and operator (for example, ministries' representatives in SOE boards; no rules for setting a majority of independent directors). However, in practice, some SOEs have a majority of independent directors (for example, SK).	• Some SOEs are exempted from government procurement procedures (for example, SK). • Similarly, favoritism in the award of public procurement has been reported.	• In theory, tax rules are the same for both public and private operators. • Yet, distortions that may appear as a result of state aid in SMEs should be further explored.	• Preferential access to finance. • Direct monetary support via subsidies, loans at privileged interest rates, and other implicit subsidies (for example, SK, Baiterek, KazAgro). • Some SOEs have preemptive rights to buy strategic facilities and bankrupt assets (for example, SK).
Benchmark	• Companies compete on a level playing field with no trade protection and market-based competition for rights to invest in state assets. • Sectors where competition is feasible are open to private investment.	• Market-based competition in public procurement. • Bids and auctions designed to reduce the risks of bid rigging.	• Tax exemptions, subsidies, and debt guarantees granted following competitive neutrality principles.	

State aid legal framework and implementation requires improvements to minimize room for anticompetitive outcomes

Level playing field in the market between SOEs and privately owned operators

Source: Borja, Pop, and Sakhonchik 2021.
Note: NPV = net present value; PSO = public service obligation; SK = Samruk-Kazyna; SMEs = small and medium enterprises; SOE = state-owned enterprise.

FIGURE 3.3

PMR scores in network sectors, Kazakhstan and comparator countries, 2018

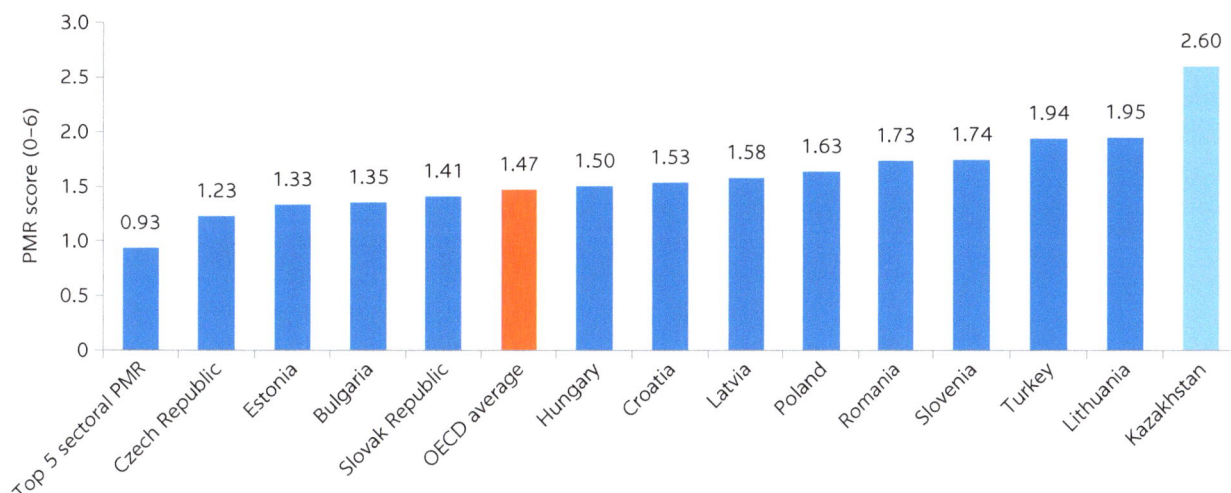

Source: Borja, Pop, and Sakhonchik 2021.
Note: The Product Market Regulation (PMR) score is an index from 0 (least restrictive) to 6 (most restrictive). The top 5 performers in the total network sector PMR are the United Kingdom, Denmark, Spain, Germany, and the Netherlands. The Organisation for Economic Co-operation and Development (OECD) average includes 35 economies. Iceland and Cyprus are omitted from the sample because of missing data on individual indicators.

telecommunications—and identifies key regulatory bottlenecks for competition, as described in the following paragraphs. This analysis of transport and telecommunications reveals that limited third-party access to essential infrastructure, other regulatory barriers to entry, and heavy public ownership play critical roles in protecting incumbents, with high costs for the economy.

Barriers to competition in the telecommunications sector are holding back digital infrastructure and the quality of digital services. The dominance of the vertically integrated state-owned operator,[12] the lack of independence of the sector regulator from the sector development agenda,[13] the limited third-party access to essential infrastructure,[14] and the absence of market-driven mechanisms to allocate radio frequency spectrum have been hindering competition and distorting the playing field for private sector operators. As a result, market outcomes remain suboptimal: data from the Global Connectivity Index suggest that Kazakhstan's digital sector infrastructure is less developed than in benchmark economics, compounded by a huge divide between rural and urban areas.[15] Moreover, the 3G and 4G penetration rates are also relatively low, with network coverage of 34.2 and 4.2 percent of the country's territory in 2019, respectively. Furthermore, the quality of services is limited, and affordability has been deteriorating.[16] At the micro level, all these factors associated with limited competition in the telecommunications sector hamper the capacity (and ability) of Kazakhstani firms to adopt new digital technologies, thereby limiting productivity payoffs. At the macro level, the underdevelopment of a broader digital economy constrains the possibility for economic diversification.

Barriers to competition in the transport and logistics sectors are increasing transportation costs, which prevents firms from exploring economies of scale and increasing productivity. Despite several liberalization efforts, the vertically integrated Kazakhstan Temir Zholy (KTZ) dominates the railway transportation sector, hampering the entry of private freight transport companies.[17] In addition, tariff regulations give rise to cross-subsidization in the rail transportation segment. By contrast, sole entrepreneurs and micro-businesses dominate the road freight transportation market. In this context, the critical bottlenecks for competition stem from tariff and nontariff barriers that limit the import of commercial trucks (supply of upstream products) and regulatory obstacles that prevent foreign entry into the insurance market. As a result, limited logistics performance and infrastructure (as reflected in the Logistics Performance Index) may be affecting the proper provision of transport services and thus transport costs for Kazakhstani firms. High transport costs constrain connectivity in the domestic market and prevent firms from increasing economies of scale, both from the supply side (by reducing input accessibility) and from the demand side (by reducing access to output markets). The net effect is to constrain firms' productivity growth.

Key priority actions to level the playing field for all companies

Removing distortions to competition in product markets would allow more productive firms to grow faster, boosting aggregate productivity. Several policy actions could reduce the restrictiveness of Kazakhstan's product market policies. Annex 3A presents the full set of recommendations to boost market competition. Among the economywide measures, the most transformational would include the following:

- Fostering competitive neutrality principles in markets[18]
- Reducing the use of noncompetitive methods for awarding procurement contracts while ensuring fairness and transparency
- Limiting the scope of price controls to market failure scenarios and for a limited period while gradually removing undue price controls in industries without clear market failures.

The government recently announced a few procompetition reforms that are somewhat aligned with the recommendations outlined above. For instance, in the aftermath of the January 2022 unrest, the authorities set forth major reforms to the Samruk-Kazyna National Welfare Fund (the Fund) that manages key SOEs and is the largest buyer of goods and services in the country. The proposed program of reforms aims, among other objectives, to reduce direct award procurement by the Fund, increasing the transparency of SOEs' procurement, reducing the state presence in the economy through initial and secondary public offerings of key network SOEs in 2022–25, and lifting barriers to access of private oil companies to oil refineries owned by the Fund. The effective implementation of these actions has yet to be seen and will require careful design and sound planning.

As for sector-specific reforms, removing competition restrictions in telecommunications and transport-logistics would have trickle-down effects on productivity growth for the whole economy.[19] Examples of procompetition reforms in these sectors include the following:

- Unbundling the vertically integrated incumbent SOEs[20]
- Strengthening the regulatory authority or separating the sector regulator from the policy-making ministry[21]
- Removing legislative bottlenecks preventing private companies from accessing key input infrastructure.[22]

RESHAPING BUSINESS SUPPORT POLICIES TO PRIORITIZE FIRM PRODUCTIVITY GROWTH RATHER THAN FIRM SURVIVAL

The government of Kazakhstan has been deploying large-scale business support programs, most of them targeting the micro, small, and medium enterprise (MSME) segment. Kazakhstan has set a long-term target of increasing the share of MSMEs in GDP to 35 percent by 2025 and 50 percent by 2050. To accomplish these objectives, the government launched several large-scale business support programs, with a specific focus on MSMEs. According to World Bank (Iootty, Bizhan, and Mamrayeva 2021), these programs encompassed financial and nonfinancial instruments and predominantly aimed to promote access to finance, capacity building, and access to technology. Table 3.1 lists key business support programs and their allocated budgets, and box 3.2 summarizes the features offered by these programs.

Despite these efforts, dynamism in the MSME sector remains low. The MSMEs in Kazakhstan comprise a large number of individual entrepreneurs and a few medium-size enterprises. They concentrate in industries with relatively low added value, such as wholesale and retail, real estate, and other services. MSMEs' contributions to employment and added value are almost half those in OECD peers. As of 2019, MSMEs accounted for only 32 percent of total added value in the economy and 37 percent of the total labor force in Kazakhstan. The analysis presented in World Bank (Iootty, Bizhan, and Mamrayeva 2021), which draws on 2019 World Bank Enterprise Survey data, shows that (1) the productivity performance of formal private MSMEs in Kazakhstan is low and has been deteriorating in the past few years, (2) MSMEs in Kazakhstan may be failing to realize the trade gains of export activities, and (3) innovation performance, adoption of digital solutions, and multiple general capabilities of private MSMEs are underdeveloped when compared with the Europe and Central Asia region average.

Although the government has more recently adopted measures to ease the impact of the COVID-19 crisis on the corporate sector, especially MSMEs, the reach of these policies was relatively limited. The MSME support measures implemented by the government of Kazakhstan since the COVID-19 outbreak

TABLE 3.1 Key business support programs: Budget envelope

PROGRAM TITLE	PROGRAM TOTAL BUDGET (BILLION KAZAKHSTANI TENGE)	SHARE OF 2020 GDP (%)
Business Roadmap	457	0.7
Economy of Simple Things	1,000	1.4
State Program for the Development of Productive Employment and Mass Entrepreneurship "Enbek"	541	0.8
State Program of Industrial and Innovative Development	781	1.1
SME Subsidized Lending Program	800	1.2
Employment Roadmap	1,000	1.4
Total	**4,579**	**6.6**

Source: Iootty, Bizhan, and Mamrayeva 2021.
Note: The programs have varying implementation periods. SME = small and medium enterprise.

BOX 3.2

Key business support programs in Kazakhstan

Prominent among the numerous business support programs available in Kazakhstan are the following:

- The Business Roadmap Program (2020–25) aims to support the private sector, including micro, small, and medium enterprises (MSMEs), through subsidized lending (up to 50 percent of loan interest payment is subsidized) and partial credit guarantees and nonfinancial measures (such as training and capacity building for entrepreneurs). Resources channeled through the ongoing second round of the program account for approximately 13 percent of the total budget of private sector support programs currently implemented in Kazakhstan.

- The Economy of Simple Things Program (2018–21) provides subsidized loans and partial credit guarantees to small and medium enterprises (SMEs) producing basic goods and services. The program envisages providing subsidized loans of any size (that is, no ceiling on loan amount) for up to 10 years at an annual interest rate of 6 percent. For partial credit guarantees, the maximum loan amount is 5 billion Kazakhstani tenge (T), of which the guarantee covers up to 50 percent for up to 10 years. As a response to the COVID-19 (coronavirus) outbreak, the program was scaled up in April 2020: the program budget has been expanded from T 600 billion to T 1 trillion (US$2.3 billion). A total of T 573 billion has been disbursed under the program since its inception in 2018.

- State Program for the Development of Productive Employment and Mass Entrepreneurship "Enbek"(2017–21) supports subsistence entrepreneurship through (1) free vocational education to youth not in employment, education, or training and self-employed middle-age citizens; (2) basic training needed for entrepreneurship (for example, principles of accounting, business planning) and subsequent microloans and microloan guarantees (up to T 16 million at a 6 percent interest rate and with a maturity of up to seven years) for microentrepreneurs and craftspeople in rural areas; and (3) subsidies and grants to support labor mobility and a national platform to match labor demand and supply. In 2020, more than 400,000 citizens

benefited from various employment support measures. In April 2020, as part of the efforts to counteract the COVID-19 pandemic, the program's budget was increased from T 30 billion to T 80 billion.

- The State Program of Industrial and Innovative Development (2020–25) is an industrial development program with an MSME support dimension. It includes local supplier development initiatives, support of six territorial clusters, business acceleration, market intelligence services for exporting MSMEs, reimbursement of export development activities, and provision of innovation vouchers to and venture financing of technological start-ups.

- The SME Subsidized Lending Program (2020–21) was launched as part of the response to the COVID-19 pandemic in March 2020. Under this program, the National Bank placed conditional deposits totaling T 800 billion at 13 commercial banks at a 5 percent annual interest rate for further onlending to SMEs. These are 12-month working capital loans at an 8 percent rate—up to T 50 million for individual entrepreneurs and up to T 3 billion for MSMEs.

- The Employment Roadmap (2020–21) program was launched in 2020 as part of the government's anticrisis measures amid the COVID-19 pandemic. The program is focused on creation of jobs through infrastructure construction and upgrade projects, including construction, overhaul and maintenance of education, health care, culture, and sports objects; housing and utilities infrastructure; engineering and transport infrastructure (roads, sidewalks, dams, bridges, water facilities, and so on); and improvement of public spaces. The project budget amounts to T 1 trillion (including T 300 billion from the republican budget and a T 700 billion bonded loan from National Management Holding Baiterek). Although the program is primarily focused on job creation through infrastructure upgrade projects, it also envisages the purchase of goods, works, and services from domestic producers. (The program requires that not less than 90 percent of a particular infrastructure project budget be spent on local goods, services, and works, if available and applicable.)

Sources: Iootty, Bizhan, and Mamrayeva 2021; Order of the Prime Minister of the Republic of Kazakhstan dated March 27, 2020, No. 55-p.

have been broadly in line with international practice. They have focused on providing liquidity and retaining jobs by expanding subsidized loans, offering partial credit guarantees, deferring or reducing taxes, and making social payments. The relief measures were particularly skewed toward activities most affected by the pandemic, such as retail trade, consumer services, and transport. The reach of the small and medium enterprise (SME) policies deployed by the government of Kazakhstan was quite limited, however. Evidence presented in World Bank (2021) shows that the share of formal private firms that received or expected to receive national or local government assistance in Kazakhstan was relatively small: 12 percent among small firms and 3 percent of medium firms. The proportion was somewhat larger among large firms at 17 percent. Overall, the fact that small and medium companies were less likely than large firms to access support suggests that policy reach was limited for the most vulnerable firms.

As the country moves to the next stage of economic recovery, it is vital that these business support programs be carefully calibrated to tackle deeper structural challenges while helping build back better so that a stronger, greener, and more inclusive economy flourishes. The speed and scale of events during the pandemic compelled policy makers to prioritize short-term challenges at the expense of long-term sustainability. As Kazakhstan moves out of the relief stage, it is important to craft state support measures to use limited fiscal resources efficiently (box 3.3). Therefore, support measures need to move from the emergency phase to a restructuring stage that prioritizes distressed but viable firms. Later, in the resilient recovery stage, business support programs should prioritize taking advantage of new market opportunities and promote the reallocation of productive resources toward long-run economic transformation. In these circumstances, support for firms' digital transformation and adoption of green technologies becomes crucial.

BOX 3.3

Adjusting the targeting criteria for business support policies

The firm-level analysis revealed a high level of heterogeneity of productivity performance in Kazakhstan (box 2.1). This result reinforces the need to design policies that go beyond the average firm. It is crucial that the types of firms that can benefit the most from a specific policy be identified. The absence of clear criteria to target the "right" firms facilitates the survival of inefficient firms.

Identifying the right criteria is not an easy task because enterprises' performance and attributes are extremely different: start-ups have different challenges and needs than established micro, small, and medium enterprises (MSMEs). Therefore, a fundamental issue

is identifying the entrepreneurs—even within MSME subgroups—that are most likely to benefit from government support by growing. As Grover, Medvedev, and Olafsen (2019) discuss, sustained MSME growth is unlikely without commensurate growth in capability. In this context, some indicators that can serve as proxies for the capacity or willingness of MSMEs to grow in productivity include investments in innovation and improving management capability, exporting activity, involvement in networks, and whether the firms have obtained external finance. All these indicators could be used to design efficiency-enhancing business support programs.

In this context, the pandemic provides an opportunity to revisit existing business support policies and pivot from firm survival to higher dynamism and productivity growth. As discussed in World Bank (Iootty, Bizhan, and Mamrayeva 2021), Kazakhstan launched most of its existing business support programs in the aftermath of the 2007–09 global financial crisis to mitigate the consequences of the domestic banking sector crunch. The government extended these support programs at least once; the justification for the extension referred to the achievement of formal program targets related to aggregate output indicators (for example, growth of the share of the manufacturing sector in GDP, growth of the number of active MSMEs, growth of MSME output). However, the programs did not prioritize any effect on (or correlation with) productivity growth nor mention potential productivity increases as a justification for continuing. As a matter of fact, the central MSME support program in Kazakhstan does not encompass explicit incentives for MSME productivity growth and contains intrinsic disincentives for MSMEs to enter new geographic and product markets that could offer higher productivity payoffs.[23]

Against this backdrop, it is crucial for Kazakhstan to move from business support programs that prioritize size-based criteria and firm survival to programs that provide incentives for firm growth and productivity increases (for example, pilot programs as described in box 3.4). To do that, the targeting criteria applied by current business support programs must be revised so that they prioritize MSME growth rather than survival (see box 3.3). Overall, a mere expansion of existing state support programs will, at best, maintain the status quo in the short term. In other words, it will perpetuate the survival of inefficient firms and will continue to lock workers into low-paying, low-productivity jobs.

The need to refocus MSME development policies is acknowledged in some of the country's key high-level development documents, including the National Development Plan of Kazakhstan until 2025 adopted in 2018 and the Roadmap for implementation of the electoral program of the Nur Otan party approved by the government of Kazakhstan in 2021. In particular, 1 of 10 national priorities declared in the National Development Plan of Kazakhstan until 2025 calls for implementation of a new approach to entrepreneurship development that covers 17 directions, including reduction of the state presence in the economy, wider use of the competitive neutrality principle, improvement of the regulatory framework, and many others.[24] In light of the above (and in accordance with the State Planning System in the Republic of Kazakhstan, approved by Government Decree No. 790, dated November 29, 2017), the authorities are currently drafting the Concept for SME Development until 2030. It is expected that the concept will define the vision for the development of entrepreneurship in Kazakhstan as well as the basic principles and approaches to the implementation of state policy, taking into account the changes to global trends and challenges resulting from the pandemic.

Key priority actions to streamline business support policies

When reviewing the MSME support strategy in Kazakhstan, it is crucial to follow best practices. Annex 3B presents the full set of suggestions. The key priority actions to guide the review of business support programs include the following:

• Conducting a public expenditure review of existing MSME support programs to scale up successful ones and redesign or discontinue those that do not work

BOX 3.4

Leveraging targeted projects to support productivity-enhancing activities in specific sectors: Some considerations

The mining industry has been one of the leading productivity drivers in Kazakhstan. Still, over time, it has begun facing challenges, including deposit depletion, deeper mines, and outdated technologies due to the volatility of global commodity prices. Avoiding further deterioration of productivity and competitiveness requires, along with global trends, a technological upgrading through the introduction of modern solutions stemming from Industry 4.0. Otherwise, at least some of the flagship industry may become deadweight.

The Autonomous Cluster Fund "Park of Innovative Technologies" or Tech Garden offers promising opportunities to tackle these challenges. It was established in 2014 as one of the two national innovation clusters in Almaty. In 2015, as part of the World Bank's technical assistance, the Tech Garden was exposed to the Chilean experience of utilizing innovation in the mining sector to develop other industries. Since then, the Tech Garden has acquired strong knowledge and experience developing and implementing Industry 4.0 projects in mining, both locally and internationally. It now represents a cluster of more than 300 companies, research institutes, and universities.

Tech Garden has developed an exciting combination of tools, such as the Smart Industry Management Platform (a platform of high-quality domestic information technology solutions for industrial enterprises that operates on "open innovation" principles), IntelliSense-LAB (a technological platform, developed with the UK, for industrial automation and digitalization for subsurface projects), and the Building Information Modelling (BIM)+ Laboratory (a platform built jointly with the US allowing digitalization of the entire life cycle of construction of objects, including industrial ones, to reduce operating costs). This capacity represents a new way of testing innovative solutions in an industrial setting—through artificial intelligence–assisted digital modeling, which has great potential to promote innovation not only in a given industry but through the entire value chain.

The government could consider more ambitious pilots going beyond the mining sector based on this model to promote digitalization and innovation in other sectors, such as transport and logistics. The Tech Garden experience suggests that the benefits of digitalization are not limited to large mining companies. Smaller technological companies, such as local suppliers, can improve their productivity and resilience as well. These pilots could also include technology consortia, cluster, and supplier development elements that have been successfully implemented under World Bank projects.

- Revisiting the targeting criteria applied by current business support programs to prioritize firm growth rather than firm survival
- Connecting business support programs with broader policies (in particular, policies supporting green growth[25] and digitalization[26])
- Introducing a robust monitoring and evaluation framework that serves as the basis for the adoption of evidence-based policies[27]
- Strengthening the institutional framework to deliver MSME policies.[28]

UNLOCKING OPPORTUNITIES FOR FOREIGN DIRECT INVESTMENT IN NONEXTRACTIVE SECTORS TO BOOST PRODUCTIVITY SPILLOVERS

Foreign direct investment (FDI) can bring many benefits to host countries and play a key role in accelerating their economic growth, increasing their participation in global value chains (GVCs), and enhancing their productivity. FDI can bring higher-skilled and better-paid jobs to host economies along with managerial skills and know-how, promote knowledge transfer, contribute to diversification, and allow for the integration of domestic firms into GVCs. The positive effects of FDI on productivity are well documented in the literature. The presence and operations of multinational corporation (MNC) affiliates can directly contribute to enhanced productivity and technology in the host economy while also supporting increases in productivity of domestic firms through spillover effects (Saurav and Kuo 2020). A country hosting FDI can experience aggregate productivity gains when MNCs use resources more efficiently (often because of modern technology). Moreover, productivity spillovers can occur through the demonstration of new technologies to domestic firms (Blomström and Kokko 1998; Kneller and Pisu 2007), through labor turnover and labor mobility between foreign and domestic firms (Görg and Strobl 2005; Poole 2013), and through interfirm links between MNC affiliates and local suppliers (Jordaan, Douw, and Qiang 2020).

Firm data in Kazakhstan suggest a productivity premium for foreign companies over their domestic peers. The analysis presented in World Bank (Jedlicka et al. 2021), drawing on 2019 World Bank Enterprise Survey data, shows that MNCs in Kazakhstan are smaller than in comparator countries but are significantly more productive than domestic firms. Data from the 2019 World Bank Enterprise Survey in Kazakhstan confirm that FDI firms enjoy a productivity premium over their domestic peers (figure 3.4). They also outperform domestic companies in technology innovation and product and service innovation (figure 3.5). These performance differences align with global evidence confirming a positive impact that MNCs can bring to host economies through improved technology and management practices and by boosting productivity growth.

Much of Kazakhstan's FDI is in the extractives sector, and the FDI links with GVCs also primarily focus on commodities, which hinders productivity spillovers. In addition to the quantity of FDI, the quality of the investments received also matters for achieving the desired economic outcomes from FDI attraction, including economic growth, productivity increases, and improved connectivity with GVCs. According to World Bank (Jedlicka et al. 2021), Kazakhstan's FDI inflows are concentrated mainly in the mining and extractives sector.[29] Based on official statistics from the National Bank, this sector attracted more than 50 percent of FDI inflows in 2015–18.[30] Professional scientific and technical activities attracted the second most investments in the same period, including investments in "geological exploration and prospecting activities," which are also closely associated with investments in the mining and extractives sector.[31] Finally, construction and wholesale and retail trade, two market-seeking sectors, attracted another significant portion of Kazakhstan's FDI inflows over the same period. Investment into export-oriented manufacturing sectors was minimal, and disinvestments exceeded investments in manufacturing-related activities overall. Because Kazakhstan's FDI inflows are mainly in mining and extractives, they are concentrated in GVCs related to commodities. The share of FDI inflows attached to commodity GVCs (more than 60 percent) is significantly higher than in regional comparator countries. Kazakhstan has managed to attract only very limited FDI in knowledge-intensive goods and services–related GVCs, which could likely bring greater economic benefits to the economy through job creation and diversification of exports.

FIGURE 3.4

MNC productivity premium over domestic firms, Kazakhstan

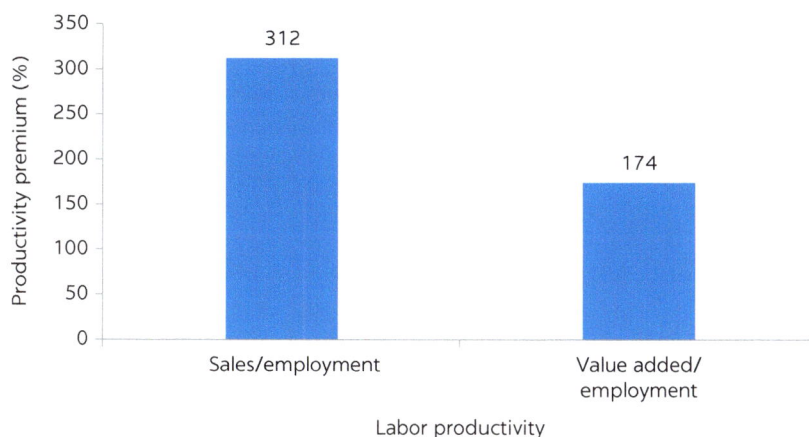

Source: Jedlicka et al. 2021.
Note: The estimated premium results from a linear regression of labor productivity explained by a dummy (domestic vs. multinational corporation [MNC]) plus firm age and sector controls. Estimated premium coefficients were statistically significant at 95 percent. A 312 percent result suggests that MNCs in Kazakhstan are, on average, 3.12 times more productive than private domestic peers (with the same age and operating in the same sector).

FIGURE 3.5

Share of firms in innovation activities, MNCs vs. domestic firms

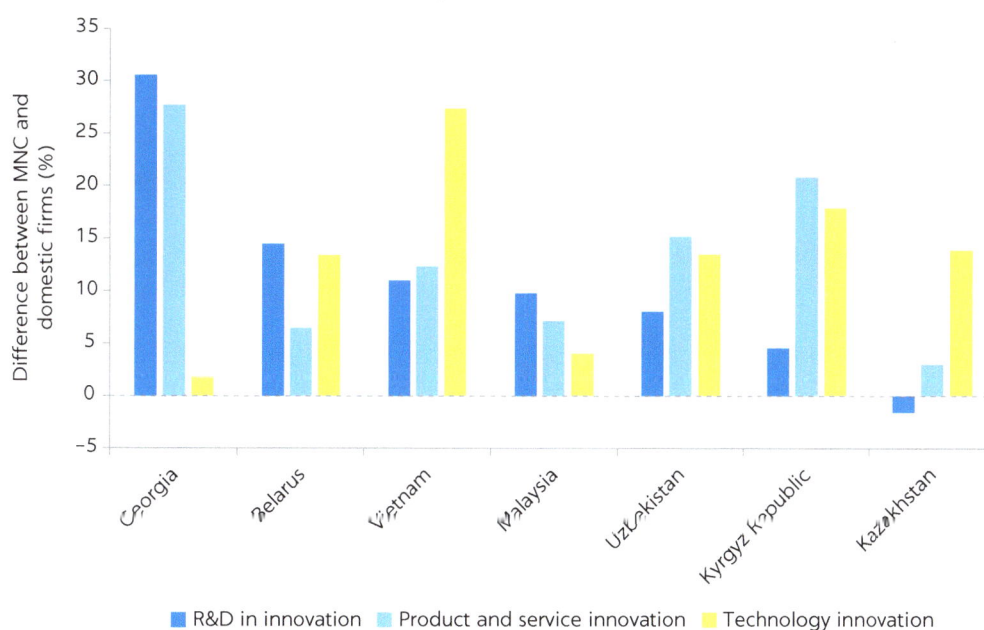

■ R&D in innovation   ■ Product and service innovation   ■ Technology innovation

Source: Jedlicka et al. 2021.
Note: MNC = multinational corporation; R&D = research and development.

The COVID-19 crisis is expected to negatively affect FDI flows globally, with the oil and gas sectors likely to be particularly affected, putting Kazakhstan at high risk for COVID-19–related effects on FDI. During the first half of 2020, new investment project announcements declined by 37 percent globally, with the largest decreases registered in the manufacturing sector. Coke and petroleum products, in particular, saw a decline of 89 percent. Greenfield FDI announcements in Kazakhstan decreased by 86 percent in the first half of 2020, which UNCTAD (2020) states could indicate "a major slowdown in future investment intentions." The country's reliance on the oil and gas sector makes its exposure to COVID-19–related FDI risks very high. Despite some recent inflows within the construction and trade sectors, the declines in new FDI project announcements could indicate a muted recovery to FDI, pointing to the need for targeted promotion of sectors contributing to diversification.

Driven by the World Trade Organization accession process, Kazakhstan has been easing FDI regulations, but the persistent concentration of FDI flows in natural resources extraction and processing sectors reveals that there are still constraints on investment. The country has moved closer to OECD standards with regard to the principle of national treatment—that is, the government is committed to treating enterprises operating on its territory but controlled by the nationals of other countries no less favorably than domestic enterprises in like situations (OECD 2021). In addition, the government has launched several initiatives to improve the quality of domestic regulations and reduce the administrative burdens faced by businesses.[32] It has also been improving the system of protection of foreign investors.[33] Last, the government has put in place a wide range of dispute resolution mechanisms.[34] Despite these recent improvements, the persistent concentration of FDI flows in natural resources extraction and processing sectors reveals that additional investment constraints are still at play. For instance, the dominant presence of SOEs in key enabling sectors—such as transport and telecommunications—combined with the absence of an independent regulatory authority in these sectors has constrained FDI attraction. Moreover, ground-level barriers in the business environment are still prevalent. World Bank (Jedlicka et al. 2021) estimates a gravity model of bilateral FDI stock using the Worldwide Governance Indicators as a measure of institutional and regulatory quality across countries. The results indicate that good institutions and an adequate regulatory environment not only make a difference in attracting FDI but also can make up for a low stage of development. Holding everything else static with regard to regulatory quality, if Kazakhstan were to catch up with Malaysia, Kazakhstan's inward FDI stock could increase by as much as 17 percent.

The need to increase and diversify Kazakhstan's FDI stock highlights the importance of having an effective investment promotion activity and a well-functioning FDI institutional framework to attract productivity-enhancing FDI. Effective investment promotion builds on three main pillars: (1) strategic alignment and focus, (2) a coherent institutional framework, and (3) excellence in investor servicing. A well-functioning FDI institutional framework requires (1) a shared strategic vision for FDI across government that includes private sector input, (2) technically capable institutions with clearly defined mandates, (3) institutional stability and sustainability through political cycles, (4) appropriate incentives for institutional cooperation with strong results measurement and communications tools, and (5) political and financial support to establish and staff institutions according to best practices. Not many countries in the developing world can claim to have all these elements in place. However, working toward these best practices will lead to a more effective institutional framework.

In this regard, there is space to improve Kazakhstan's institutional framework for FDI attraction. According to the diagnostic presented in World Bank

(Jedlicka et al. 2021), multiple institutions are involved in investment policy formulation and execution in Kazakhstan, and their relationships and collaboration leave room for improvement. The MNE is responsible for investment policy formulation, while its implementation is the responsibility of the Ministry of Foreign Affairs and its Investment Committee. Kazakh Invest, the implementing agency, reports to the Investment Committee through a service contract. Separating investment policy making and implementation into different institutions is good practice. However, there must be clear and well-defined coordination mechanisms between the institutions. Best practice separates the "upstream" function of developing and formulating policies from "downstream" implementation; typically, a government ministry is responsible for upstream policy making, and an operational agency conducts the downstream implementation. Usually, this would be an investment promotion agency reporting to the same ministry. In addition, several high-level consulting bodies have been created in Kazakhstan to tackle various aspects of the investment climate without apparent coordination of their activities. The regional dimension adds to the overall complexity because only Kazakh Invest has formal regional representation not based on official collaboration documents with akimats (subnational governments). This ambiguity leaves room for duplication of functions (such as investment promotion by regional authorities) and the diffusion of responsibility when dealing with investor grievances and aftercare.

Key priority areas to create favorable conditions for attracting, retaining, and expanding FDI

Against this backdrop, Kazakhstan will need to strengthen the effectiveness of its institutional framework for FDI to attract more and higher-quality investments. Pressing reforms include the following (annex 3C presents the full set of recommendations):

- Reviewing sector priorities for FDI attraction
- Revising the mandate of Kazakh Invest to focus primarily on investment promotion (rather than on business regulatory functions)
- Introducing key performance indicators to Kazakh Invest for measuring the success of its investment promotion efforts
- Establishing an effective national-subnational framework for coordinating the investment promotion activities of Kazakh Invest and the akimats
- Enhancing institutional coordination mechanisms between the policy makers (ministries) and implementing agencies (Kazakh Invest) of Kazakhstan's investment attraction and retention policies.

In September 2021, the government initiated development of the Investment Policy Concept for the Republic of Kazakhstan until 2025. The main goal of this policy is to create favorable conditions for the activities of foreign and domestic investors. The concept envisages an ambitious array of investment climate reforms to enhance the country's investment competitiveness for the attraction, retention, and expansion of foreign and domestic investments. Among the reforms to be included in this concept are measures aimed at strengthening investor aftercare by improving coordination between central and regional authorities, investors, and the national investment promotion agency (Kazakh Invest).

BOOSTING R&D AND INNOVATION TO MAXIMIZE THE IMPACT ON PRODUCTIVITY

Kazakhstan's gross expenditure on research and development (R&D) as a share of GDP is below what would be expected, and the country has a low level of translation of R&D expenditures into patents. As discussed in World Bank (Slavova and Rubalcaba 2021), Kazakhstan is underinvesting in R&D; its gross expenditure on R&D as a share of GDP is systematically below what would be expected given its level of economic development (figure 3.6). The indicator is also much lower than in other natural resource–intensive countries, including Australia and Canada, and at about 10 percent of the Republic of Korea's investment level when that country was at a similar level of development.

In addition, Kazakhstan demonstrates a comparatively low level of translation of R&D into patents, which might indicate both low-quality research and market and institutional failures in the process of turning research results into patents. In particular, despite the relatively large number of organizations and personnel engaged in R&D, the number of patents significantly lags behind peer countries. As figure 3.7 demonstrates, the number of patents per researcher, a proxy for innovativeness, is also low compared with the average and with Korea, when controlling for the country's development level. These findings raise questions about the productivity of workers, the efficiency of processes involved in R&D, and the quality of research and innovations in Kazakhstan.

It is also possible that R&D organizations practice the overstaffing from which most state-owned organizations suffer around the globe. R&D personnel may be shouldered with unproductive and bureaucratic activities unrelated to creating new and original ideas, and capital or human resources could be misallocated, preventing them from fulfilling their true potential.

This subdued performance at the macro level reflects unsatisfactory performance at the micro level given that the share of innovative firms in Kazakhstan is not large, especially among MSMEs. The lack of innovativeness of existing firms is also closely related to the small percentage of knowledge-intensive start-ups and business investments in R&D. For instance, analysis presented in World Bank (Slavova and Rubalcaba 2021) drawing on 2019 World Bank Enterprise Survey data shows that only 2.1 percent of formal private firms in Kazakhstan spend on R&D, about four times lower than the Europe and Central Asia region average. Only 22.7 percent of formal private firms have introduced product, service, or process innovations. The gap with Europe and Central Asia region averages is driven by small (5–19 employees) and medium (20–99 employees) firms; it virtually disappears for large firms. For example, the share of large firms in Kazakhstan that use foreign-licensed technology is almost double the Europe and Central Asia region average. The low innovation among SMEs in Kazakhstan is partly due to the concentration of private SMEs in retail and services that have little demand for innovation because of the generally short-term nature of the business and lack of capital. In addition, small businesses in the country often prefer to remain small to avoid moving to a different, more complicated tax and regulatory regime.

The innovation policy mix in Kazakhstan combines various instruments that replicate the organizational structures and best practices of developed countries, but the linking of these instruments to the private sector and the general framework conditions leave significant room for improvement. In particular, for the pre-R&D planning and fundamental research stages, the country has established the Supreme Science and Technology Commission under the prime minister

FIGURE 3.6
National R&D expenditure comparison

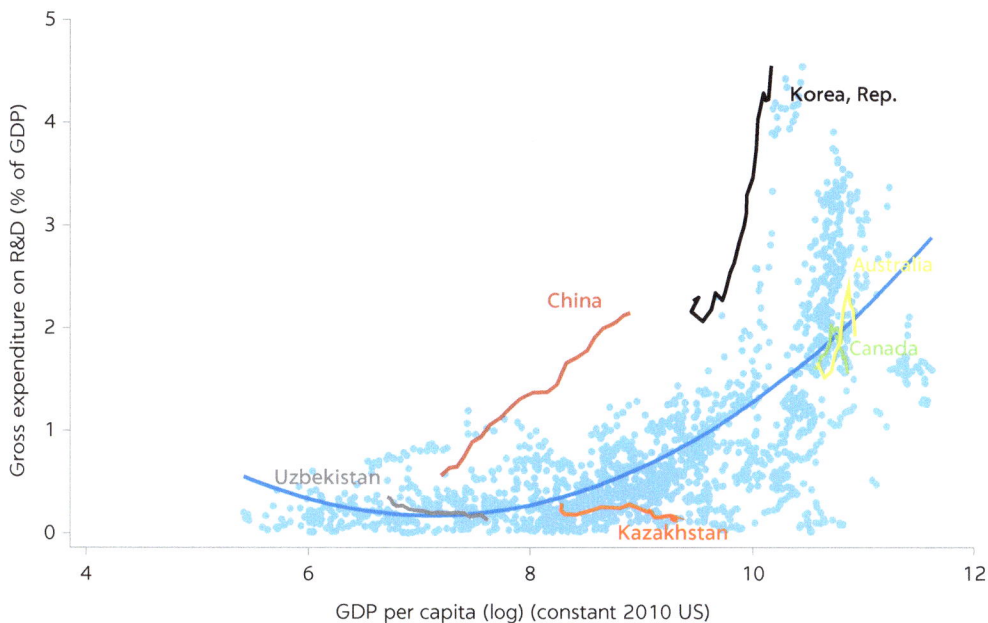

Source: Slavova and Rubalcaba 2021.
Note: The earliest data on gross research and development (R&D) expenditure and GDP per capita are available for 1996. Data for both gross expenditure on R&D (%) and GDP per capita for Kazakhstan are available for 1997–2018; Uzbekistan 2000–18; Korea, Rep. 1996–2017; Canada 1996–2018; China 1996–2017; Australia 1996, 1998, 2000, 2002, 2004, 2006, 2008, 2010, 2011, 2013, 2015.

FIGURE 3.7
Patents per researcher and GDP per capita

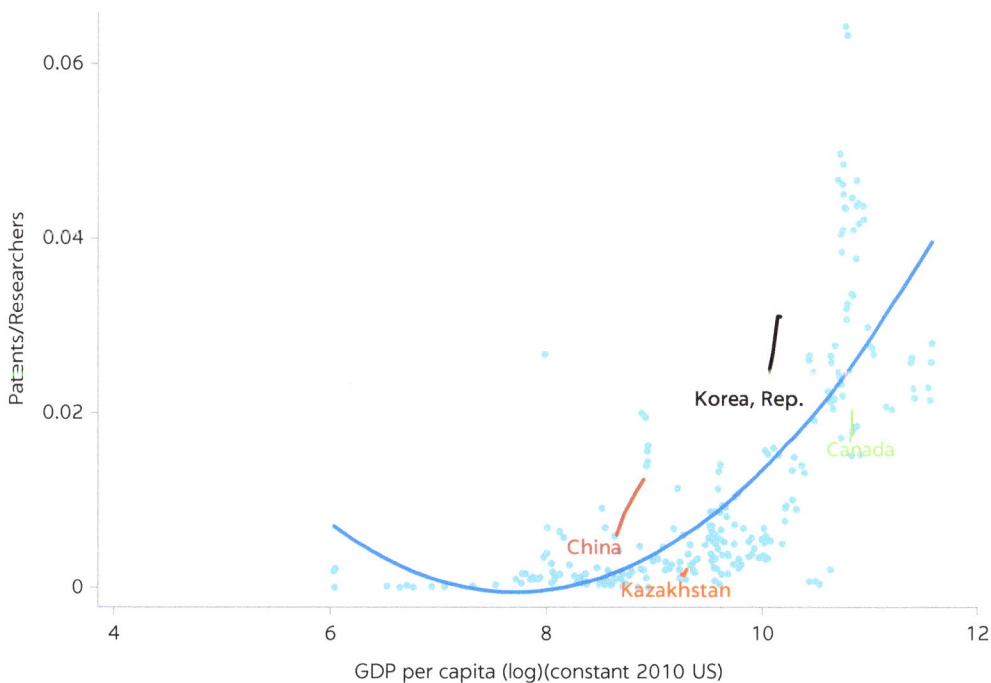

Source: Slavova and Rubalcaba 2021.
Note: The earliest data on gross research and development (R&D) expenditure and GDP per capita are available for 1996. Data for both gross expenditure on R&D (%) and GDP per capita for Kazakhstan are available for 1997–2018; Uzbekistan 2000–18; Korea, Rep. 1996–2017; Canada 1996–2018; China 1996–2017; Australia 1996, 1998, 2000, 2002, 2004, 2006, 2008, 2010, 2011, 2013, 2015.

and national scientific councils designated to identify technological needs of the industry and match public research organization (PRO) and university research efforts to those needs. However, although industry representatives are present on these councils, the challenge remains to link decisions of the councils to industry needs given the lack of permanent dialogue with the private sector. Beyond the R&D stage, the country has also established several entities (Science Fund, Astana Hub, Sovereign Cluster Fund, CETT, QazTech Ventures, and several incubators) focused on pre-seed funding, seed investment, and nonfinancial support of innovative projects and knowledge start-ups. These instruments follow the global experience of public investment in knowledge creation and accumulation of a critical mass of knowledge start-ups. At the same time, the linking of these instruments to private sector needs and the general framework conditions is weak,[35] and there is little history of collaborative projects between science and industry (box 3.5 compares Kazakhstan's R&D performance to that of other countries).

BOX 3.5

Brief insights into quality of research in Kazakhstan

Kazakhstan has sound scientific and technical potential, although the transformation of registered patents into new commercial products is limited, suggesting failures at the commercialization stage. Countries should look beyond immediate wins and align research and development (R&D)—and hence innovation—efforts with long-term strategic goals to become front-runners in innovation. In this regard, patents and patent citations are increasingly used as measures of innovation performance, especially when it addresses technologically radical innovation (Katila 2000, 2007). According to Kenzhaliyev et al. (2020), there is a paradox in Kazakhstan today: although the scientific and technical potential is high (as measured by the level of infrastructure, institutions, and GDP per capita), the commercialization of scientific research is low (for example, compared with world leaders, such as the United States). While universities and research institutes produce scientific patents, there is no effective introduction of patents and scientific discoveries into production.

Kazakhstan is among the countries with the lowest R&D expenditure and patent applications per million population. Intellectual property laws and regulations (covering ownership rights over patents, copyrights,

and trademarks) allow the adoption of temporary technological rents and affect the incentives to generate knowledge. Khan and Cox (2017) refer to various methods for operationalizing a nation's capacity for innovation. These measures include royalty and license fees, trademarks, patents, and the adoption of new technological products. Other traditional measures of innovation—apart from R&D expenditures—include the number of people with PhDs, research articles, research centers created, and patents issued (patent intensity). Figure B3.5.1 depicts gross expenditure on R&D and Patent Cooperation Treaty patent registrations per million population, with Sweden and Finland at the top of the ranking. Kazakhstan performs poorly on this measure, ranking among the countries with the lowest levels of R&D expenditure and patent applications (Schwab and Zahidi 2020). This outcome could be a consequence of the fact that research work mainly aims at fulfilling formal requirements rather than being transformed into commercially viable products. As a result, according to Zhanbayev et al. (2020), most research outcomes do not find effective applications and do not contribute to the progress of the national economy via the commercialization of scientific results.

(Continued)

Box 3.5, *continued*

Gross expenditure on R&D and Patent Cooperation Treaty patents, Europe and Central Asia Region, 2017

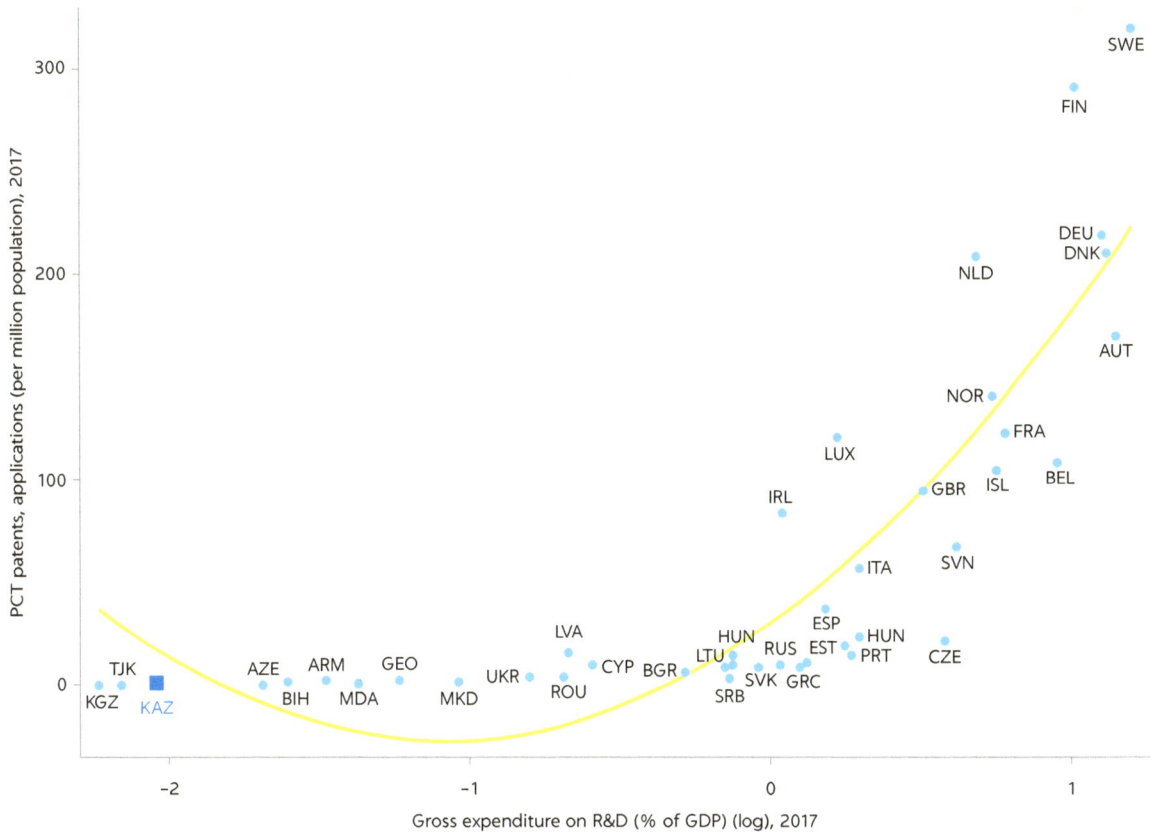

Source: Slavova and Rubalcaba 2021.
Note: PCT = Patent Cooperation Treaty; R&D = research and development.

The national innovation system (NIS) remains fragmented, with little coordination among numerous actors, which aggravates the lack of market relevance of public-funded R&D. World Bank (Slavova and Rubalcaba 2021) assesses the country's innovation performance through the lenses of an NIS.[36] The analysis shows that Kazakhstan's innovation system remains fragmented because of a multiplicity of overlapping strategies and programs related to different policy actors in the system. On the policy design and coordination level, three ministries (the Ministry of Digital Development, Innovation and Aerospace Industry [MDDIAI], the Ministry of Education and Science [MoES], and the Ministry of Industry and Infrastructural Development [MIID]) are key actors. Several line ministries, autonomous innovation clusters, and national holdings accompany them. Each of the three key ministries has one or more innovation support platforms, each having its own specialization. In particular, the MDDIAI oversees joint-stock company (JSC) National Infocommunication Holding Zerde, which in turn owns three JSCs (National Information Technologies, International Technopark of IT Startups AstanaHub, and Center for Engineering and Technology Transfer). The MoES oversees the Science Fund, most universities, and some research institutes. MIID oversees the JSC Kazakhstan Industry and Export Center (QazIndustry), an operator of industrial development programs, including Industry 4.0 initiatives. The presence of numerous public actors hampers coordination and cooperation between the main programs and affiliated institutions. The result is inefficient utilization of already scarce public resources. For example, agencies compete for administrative resources and budget, and heavy support of inefficient firms hampers the reallocation of resources to the most efficient and innovative firms.

The fragmentation of the policy delivery structure constrains opportunities for science-industry collaboration, which constrains productivity growth. In an ideal setting, knowledge from universities and laboratories transfers to the enterprise sector, leading to new or improved products and services and helping firms enter new markets and increase productivity growth. In Kazakhstan, this process, known as technology transfer or technology commercialization, faces certain institutional failures due to the fragmentation mentioned above. In particular, the lack of coordination at the policy design and implementation stages makes industry needs opaque to the NIS actors that oversee basic and applied research. These include PROs under the MoES, the Ministry of Healthcare, the Ministry of Agriculture, universities, and other bodies. The PROs also follow the usual linear innovation model with well-defined stages (research, patent and publication, prototyping, and introduction into industry).

The lack of interaction with industry at any stage of this linear model creates two mutually reinforcing issues. First, the PROs rely heavily on the state budget at each stage of the linear model, which results in reliance on performance indicators disconnected from market needs and the prioritization of administrative aims. Second, the PROs lack an understanding of the needs of the private sector, which results in a lack of private funding for R&D commercialization (cementing PROs' dependence on public funding). Hence, PROs tend to focus on research excellence and lack R&D commercialization capacity. The actors overseeing the "demand" side of the NIS (that is, MIID, MDDIAI, innovation clusters, Baiterek Holding) have their own isolated policy agendas geared toward maintaining the status quo in industrial sectors of the economy. Often, this implies continued state support and limitation of competition (for example, tariffs and nontariff barriers to automobile imports, long-term offtake contracts for local producers). Hence, a number of sectors of the economy focus on factor-driven growth rather than innovation-driven growth, resulting in the lack of R&D commercialization capacity on the demand side. As a result, PROs can often only provide a laboratory-tested technology that cannot be safely tested in an industrial setting, while industrial enterprises lack the capacity and long-term strategy to engage with local PROs and prefer packaged solutions from abroad.

Government efforts to encourage innovation by nurturing start-ups have been limited by the risk aversion of the state institutions that run them. The government of Kazakhstan launched several initiatives to nurture knowledge-based start-ups (for example, technoparks, innovation clusters, financial and nonfinancial support programs). Because of the small number of private investors who are ready to work with R&D teams and start-ups at the earliest stages of development, these kinds of initiatives can play an important role in shaping the deal flow for investors at the later stages of start-up development. However, the state institutions involved are subject to heavy reporting requirements and tend to concentrate only on carefully selected projects with well-established sales because of the risk aversion of public fund managers. As a result, most projects focus on niche markets with modest volume, which are rarely attractive to private investors at the later stages of venture financing.

Key priority actions to streamline STI policies

As a practical next step to address the challenges of the NIS, the government of Kazakhstan could consider improving the coordination between NIS stakeholders and addressing the framework conditions that hamper industry-science links. In particular, the government of Kazakhstan needs to improve the management of policy design to enhance the complementarity of existing innovation support policies and address duplication and coordination failures between innovation support programs and the numerous regional development, industrial development, and SME support programs. It could achieve this by implementing a set of reforms (annex 3D presents the complete list of suggested recommendations):

- Establishing a trusted platform for the impartial monitoring and evaluation of the effectiveness of the NIS and different public and private initiatives within it
- Expanding SMEs' capabilities to develop or adapt innovations by improving management consulting services to SMEs
- Spreading the adoption of productive technologies by scaling up existing pilots on innovative consortia activities
- Ensuring that selection of R&D teams and start-ups within the framework of support programs is based on commercialization potential.

In October 2021, the government announced a few reforms that are aligned with some of the recommendations listed above. Specifically, the national project "Technological Breakthrough through Digitalization, Science and Innovation," approved by Government Decree No. 727 of October 12, 2021, envisages the establishment of the Innovation Observatory to improve coordination of NIS stakeholders. However, the government has yet to determine mechanisms to operationalize the Innovation Observatory (for example, which state agency will host it and how to ensure its proper staffing and financing).

TACKLING KEY IMPLEMENTATION CHALLENGES

Implementing such a wide-ranging set of productivity reforms will require strong institutional coordination. The proposed reforms span multiple policy areas and stakeholders. Their implementation will require efficient coordination. In the end, the quality of government action will depend on four key drivers: the overall rationale and design of the policy, the efficacy of the implementation, the coherence of policies across various actors, and the consistency and predictability of policy over time. Despite its ambitious targets for productivity growth, Kazakhstan lacks a coordination mechanism to lead the implementation of several line policies. Such a structure would help identify and address the current policies' gaps and help coordinate and prioritize intervention. Presently, Kazakhstan has numerous policies and strategies that touch upon productivity-related drivers, such as MSMEs, innovation, FDI, and competition. However, the responsibility for implementing these various national policies, strategies, and programs is dispersed across many public sector institutions with conflicting mandates and policy goals. This fragmentation creates information silos within each government area, which might restrict the quality of a productivity-enhancing policy and the magnitude of potential economic gains. In this context, the coordination of institutions at various levels needs to be strengthened to ensure the appropriate implementation of productivity-enhancing policies. Establishing an overarching productivity council that oversees the overall functioning of the various government bodies and line ministries and that spans elected administrations might mitigate the coordination problems. This type of arrangement should have legitimacy and weight within the public debate to build awareness among critical stakeholders regarding current policy problems and the potential payoffs associated with policy change. There are many successful examples of national productivity councils or agencies, such as the Australian Productivity Commission, created in 1998, and the Mexican National Productivity Committee, created in 2013.

This extensive reform process would also be accompanied by political processes of varying complexity and cost and would require political economy support. The incentives embedded in the business environment define the relative payoffs for entrepreneurship, rent-seeking, or outright bribery. They, therefore, affect an economy's growth potential and dynamism (Baumol 1990). The suggested reforms aim to boost market functioning and change the economy's incentive structure to maximize entrepreneurship returns and diminish incentives for rent-seeking. Therefore, some of these policies will challenge the incumbent interests and may face resistance. There will also be coordination costs. The reduced version of the policy matrix outlined in the executive summary—and the extended version presented in the annexes to this chapter—highlight some of the expected costs and implementation challenges.

To address coordination and political economy costs, building consensus using sound empirical evidence is crucial. In this light, the analysis developed under the "Joint Economic Research Program (JERP) Technical Assistance to Support Productivity Growth in Kazakhstan" provides a strong analytical underpinning, connects the proposed reforms with a broader productivity agenda, and is expected to help build stakeholder buy-in and consensus about the need for reforms.

ANNEX 3A: POLICY OPTIONS TO REMOVE ECONOMYWIDE AND SECTOR-SPECIFIC BARRIERS TO COMPETITION

TABLE 3A.1 Policy options to remove economywide and sector-specific barriers to competition

KEY AREAS	PRIORITY	RESPONSIBLE ACTOR(S)	IMPLEMENTATION CHALLENGES
Economywide			
1. Consider refocusing SOEs' direct participation in areas where private sector solutions and financing are not feasible. Private sector participation could be promoted in these sectors through public-private partnerships to increase competitive pressure.	Medium term	MoF, MNE	Refocusing SOEs' direct participation might be challenging in sectors and geographic locations that are less appealing for the private sector (for example, utilities services in small towns or rural areas). Public-private partnerships for providing basic public services may experience regulatory risks (for example, politically driven tariff ceilings in the transport sector, absence of rules on access to confidential data in the health care sector, and so forth).
2. Foster competitive neutrality principles in markets by (1) requiring a clear separation between commercial and noncommercial activities of SOEs, (2) mandating that SOEs earn rates of return comparable to private sector competitors, (3) limiting conflicting roles of the state as regulator and operator in certain sectors, and (4) ensuring full debt and regulatory liability of SOEs.	Short term	MoF, MNE	The process of fostering competitive neutrality principles may be hampered by the presence of high-ranking government officials in SOEs' boards causing a risk of political interference in SOE operations to prevent price or tariff hikes for goods or services that have previously been cross-subsidized.
3. Consider reducing the use of noncompetitive methods for awarding procurement contracts, ensuring fairness and transparency.	Short term	MoF	Because procurement by major SOEs is regulated by a separate law and SOEs' internal rules, the key challenge is the lack of accountability of SOEs' management.
4. Consider limiting the scope of price controls to market failure scenarios and for a limited time, while gradually removing undue price controls in industries without clear market failures that need to be addressed.	Medium term	MNE, line ministries	The lack of strong political championship and the lack of broad public discussion and consensus-building on price liberalization are key challenges.
Sector specific			
A. Telecommunications			
5. Strengthen competition advocacy by conducting market studies on barriers to competition in the telecom sector.	Medium term	Competition Protection and Development Agency	Lack of budget and political independence of the competition agency. The lack of sector-specific expertise in the competition agency.

(Continued)

TABLE 3A.1, *continued*

KEY AREAS	PRIORITY	RESPONSIBLE ACTOR(S)	IMPLEMENTATION CHALLENGES
A. Telecommunications			
6. Proactively engage in investigation of cases of refusal to share key infrastructure to ensure effective implementation of the existing third-party access rules, allowing new operators to access essential infrastructure.	Medium term	Committee for Telecommunications of the MDDIAI	Regulator's potential vulnerability to ministry or other government interference and to lobbying by the incumbent operator.
7. Consider establishing working groups with all key stakeholders to discuss the formulation of key policies for the telecom sector, for example, the strategic plan for rolling out 5G networks (currently, the formulation of a national 5G rollout plan is solely led by Kazakhtelecom).	Medium term	MDDIAI	The lack of consensus-building efforts by the MDDIAI and transaction costs of such efforts.
8. Consider unbundling the two mobile operators (Mobile Telecom-Service LLP and Kcell JSC) that had originally been separate companies and preparing them for privatization.	Short term	Prime Minister's Office	Diseconomies of scale may cause higher average cost of mobile communication services. The unbundling may result in higher capital and operational expenditures by the two operators.
9. Consider unbundling Kazakhtelecom into a wholesale arm and a retail arm to introduce more transparency and eliminate internal cross-subsidies.	Short term	Prime Minister's Office	Political economy issues may lead to broadband tariff hikes in the short term.
10. Consider further divestiture of state shares in state-owned telecom operators to attract private investment.	Medium term	Prime Minister's Office	The saturation of the mobile communication market reduces potential benefits of investments in the sector. The divestiture will require amendments to the Law on National Security, which requires foreign investors to obtain a government waiver to acquire more than 49 percent of shares of major telecom operators, including incumbent operator Kazakhtelecom.
11. Consider passing legislation to strengthen the regulatory authority for the telecommunications sector (the Telecommunications Committee of the MDDIAI) and separate the sector regulator (the Telecommunications Committee of the MDDIAI) from the policy-making ministry (the MDDIAI).	Medium term	Competition Protection and Development Agency, MDDIAI, Parliament	Because decisions of a regulator may have significant economic impacts on various stakeholders, strengthening the authority of the telecom regulator may evoke resistance from business entities and public institutions. As a result, this may become a lengthy political process as well as bring about transaction costs.
12. Consider removing existing access restrictions to underutilized fiber-optic networks managed by private real estate management companies, public utilities, and telecom operators with significant market power. Consider introducing open-access regulations to manage conditions of access, capacity allocation, access pricing, nondiscrimination, and dispute resolution.	Short term	MDDIAI	Legislative bottlenecks that prevent co-deployment of telecom infrastructure along with nontelecom utilities through harmonization of a number of laws (governing telecom, energy, transport, construction, utilities sectors) and related by-laws and rules.
13. Consider removing entry restrictions in the cross-border connec-tivity market.	Short term	MDDIAI	The key challenge is the political process of amending the laws on communication and national security that limit entry to the cross-border connectivity market.

(Continued)

TABLE 3A.1, *continued*

KEY AREAS	PRIORITY	RESPONSIBLE ACTOR(S)	IMPLEMENTATION CHALLENGES
A.1 Fixed communication, fixed broadband internet			
14. Consider introducing ex ante resale obligations for operators with significant market power.	Short term	Committee for Telecommunications of the MDDIAI, Competition Protection and Development Agency	Requires strengthening the independence of the regulator in view of the regulator's potential vulnerability to ministry and other government interference and to lobbying by the incumbent operator.
15. Consider passing regulations to encourage infrastructure sharing of fiber-optic backbone capacity, passive and active infrastructure, and access to essential facilities (including those managed by public utilities). Consider stipulating ir discriminate access of telecom operators to premises of real estate objects n urban areas.	Medium term	MDDIAI	Requires better coordination between MDDIAI, regional authorities, and utility and construction companies. This might be a time- and resource-consuming process.
A.2 Mobile communication, mobile broadband internet			
16. Consider updating spectrum management rules to allow for the assignment of available spectrum for 4G (or 5G), spectrum trading, re-farming, and dynamic use. Charge market-based price for radio frequency spectrum and use the resources to provide incentives for network sharing by operators.	Medium term	MDDIAI	Requires strengthening the independence of the regulator in view of the regulator's potential vulnerability to ministry or other government interference and to lobbying by the incumbent operator.
B. Transport			
17. Ensure greater independence of the Committee on Regulation of Natural Monopolies under the Ministry of National Economy to investigate anticompetitive practices (including by SOEs).	Medium term	Prime Minister's Office	Institutional resistance by the Ministry of National Economy presents a key challenge. In addition, ensuring greater independence of the committee will entail amendments to a number of laws and by-laws, which might be challenging even in the medium term.
18. Consider passing legislation to strengthen the regulatory authority for the transport sector (the Transport Committee of the MIID) and separate the sector regulator (Transport Committee of the MIID) from the policy-making ministry (MIID).	Medium term	Competition Protection and Development Agency, MIID, Parliament	Because decisions of a regulator may have significant economic impacts on various stakeholders, strengthening the authority of the transport regulator may evoke resistance from business entities and public institutions. As a result, this may become a lengthy political process as well as bring about high transaction costs.
19. Consider harmonizing procedures and policies for cross-border operations to reduce travel time and costs of road transport services.	Medium term	Prime Minister's Office	Infrastructure bottlenecks, aggravated by seasonality of certain commodity exports (for example, grain) and seasonal surpluses or shortages of the rolling stock in bordering countries may hinder efficient cross-border operations.

(Continued)

TABLE 3A.1, *continued*

KEY AREAS	PRIORITY	RESPONSIBLE ACTOR(S)	IMPLEMENTATION CHALLENGES
B.1 Railway sector			
20. Consider separating coordination and organization function of access to mainline railway network from KTZ Express's freight-forwarding business.	Medium term	MIID	Ensuring de facto separation of coordination function of KTZ Express may be challenging without independence of the sector regulator from MIID or divestiture of KTZ Express from KTZ.
21. Consider strengthening vertical separation (in particular, well-enforced accounting separation) between KTZ's operations along the value chain to avoid cross-subsidizing or transfer of funds into segments open to competitors.	Short term	Committee on Regulation of Natural Monopolies under the MNE, MIID	Potential resistance to the separation referring to diseconomies of scope and efficiency loss.
22. Consider removing financially burdensome noncore obligations imposed on KTZ.	Short term	Prime Minister's Office, NWF Samruk-Kazyna	The presence of high-ranking government officials on the KTZ board presents a risk of political interference and imposition of social obligations on the SOE.
23. Consider strengthening regulatory oversight and capacity of the Committee on Regulation of Natural Monopolies under the Ministry of National Economy to set tariff schedules.	Short term	Prime Minister's Office	The absence of political championship and price hikes for essential social goods (for example, coal, grain) expected with market-based tariff schedules present challenges.
24. Consider divesting KTZ Express completely to prevent the risk of exclusionary practices.	Medium term	MIID	Potential resistance to the separation referring to diseconomies of scope and efficiency loss.
B.2 Trucking sector			
25. Consider removing restrictions on input products (import of trucks) and services (entry of foreign insurance companies) that limit entry and expansion of trucking companies.	Medium term	Prime Minister's Office	The proposed action would be a major change of protective policies in the automobile subsector, which is expected to counteract via lobbying groups, including lobbying by the country's major trade partners within the framework of the Eurasian Economic Union.

Source: World Bank.

Note: KTZ = Kazakhstan Temir Zholy; MDDIAI = Ministry of Digital Development, Innovation and Aerospace Industry; MIID = Ministry of Industry and Infrastructural Development; MNE = Ministry of National Economy; MoF = Ministry of Finance; NWF = National Welfare Fund; SOEs = state-owned enterprises; 4G = fourth-generation mobile network; 5G = fifth-generation mobile network.

ANNEX 3B: POLICY OPTIONS TO RESHAPE BUSINESS SUPPORT PROGRAMS

TABLE 3B.1 **Policy options to reshape business support programs**

KEY AREAS	PRIORITY	RESPONSIBLE ACTOR(S)	KEY IMPLEMENTATION CHALLENGES
1. Conduct a public expenditure review of existing MSME support programs to scale up successful ones and redesign or discontinue those that do not work.	Short term	MNE, MoF, MIID, regional akimats,[a] Bureau of National Statistics	Public expenditure review will require a comprehensive set of data on inputs and outputs of at least five major support programs. Because the programs were launched as far back as 2010 under overlapping and uncoordinated initiatives, attribution of beneficiaries' performance to programs' activities poses a major challenge.
2. Move away from business support programs that prioritize only size-based criteria to programs that provide incentives for firm growth and productivity increases. Consider revisiting the targeting criteria applied by current business support programs so that MSME growth, rather than survival, is prioritized.	Short term	MNE, MoF, MIID, Prime Minister's Office, Administration of the President, Parliament, National Bank	Because the existing support programs and size-based policies are "too large to close," the move to new support programs with fundamentally different development objectives will need to be gradual to allow MSMEs to adjust. Retaining political championship during this period might be challenging.
3. Introduce a robust monitoring and evaluation framework that serves as the basis for adoption of evidence-based policies. • *Strengthening SME data and statistics collection and analytical capacity* • *Broadening the scope of indicators to be monitored.* In addition to standard indicators such as disbursement of funds and number of beneficiary firms, it is important to measure intermediate outcomes such as firms reporting new management practices, new production processes, and quality control practices, and performance indicators such as growth in sales or output, exports, investment, productivity, and so on.	Short term	State Revenue Committee, Bureau of National Statistics	Strengthening SME data collection and analysis will require a major coordination effort between the statistics bureau and the tax authorities. The two public offices combined produce more than 150 data reports with varying periodicity and targeting various types of activities; some of these reports collect the same information. Streamlining existing reporting requirements may offset SMEs' reporting burden from new indicators.
4. Consider revisiting the wider set of size-based policies (for example, taxation regime and inspection moratoriums); they are likely to generate perverse effects by encouraging firms to stay small and do not bring concrete results for productivity growth	Medium term	MNE, MoF	Revisiting size-based policies may result in closure of inefficient SMEs in the short term; hence, successful revisiting of such policies requires a challenging consensus-building process among the broad public at the design stage and strong political championship at the implementation stage.

(Continued)

TABLE 3B.1, *continued*

KEY AREAS	PRIORITY	RESPONSIBLE ACTOR(S)	KEY IMPLEMENTATION CHALLENGES
5. Consider redesigning MSME support policies connecting with broader policies. • *Connecting MSMEs to green growth strategy.* Consider developing proactive instruments to help MSMEs adapt to new environmental regulations and to create, adopt, and sell low-carbon and energy-efficient technologies or services through the development of information-sharing platforms, implementation of a green financing mechanism, and introduction of "green" certification criteria for public procurement purposes. • *Connecting MSMEs to digital transition.* Consider implementing specific measures to accelerate the adoption of digital technologies by MSMEs (for example, provide one-time marketing consultancy or training vouchers, help MSMEs access cloud computing and purchase cloud technology, promote awareness campaigns to decrease distrust toward e-commerce practices, and provide comprehensive information and guidelines to MSMEs on regulations related to e-commerce in Kazakhstan and its key trading partners).	Medium term	MNE	Coordination of a large number of stakeholders involved in redesigning and connecting MSME policies with broader policies may present a major challenge. A particular challenge is building MSMEs' capacity to adopt digital technologies and the absence of connectivity in rural areas and small towns.
6. Consider redesigning MSME support policies grouping instruments into strategic areas. • *Access to markets.* – Ensure efficient and open public procurement policies so all firms—including MSMEs—can participate, without necessarily setting MSME quotas (for example, developing an e-procurement system and offering training to MSMEs on procurement rules and standards). – Boost entry of Kazakhstani MSMEs into global markets (for example, supplier development programs to link MSMEs to larger firms and multinationals, and export development programs to provide information on regulation and quality standards in targeted export markets).	Medium term	MNE, MoF, MIID, regional akimats, National Bank	Political championship and intensive coordination are required to ensure buy-in by major stakeholders (SOEs and multinational companies) to involve more MSMEs in their supply chains. Apart from the possible resistance of the existing provider of TA programs, the short-term challenge is the low absorption capacity of the private business development services market. The presence of substantial subsidized lending programs is a major challenge for introducing market-oriented policies. The corresponding revision of existing lending programs might trigger strong opposition from the banking sector. In the short to medium term, the discontinuation of subsidized lending may result in a wave of bankruptcies of inefficient firms.

(Continued)

TABLE 3B.1, *continued*

KEY AREAS	PRIORITY	RESPONSIBLE ACTOR(S)	KEY IMPLEMENTATION CHALLENGES
• *Firm capabilities.* Revisit existing programs that support firm capabilities to allow for a larger uptake and impact (for example, reducing the role of supply-driven TA programs through the gradual introduction of cofinancing by MSMEs in the short term and replacing the state-funded TA with a private business development services market in the medium term). • *Access to finance.* Go beyond subsidized lending and tackle market-oriented policies to address risks and transaction costs associated with lending to foster MSMEs' access to finance. For example, promote the development of an efficient and inclusive credit infrastructure (credit bureaus and movable collateral registries), fintech solutions, and well-designed partial credit guarantees.			
7. Strengthen the institutional framework to deliver MSME policies. • *Strengthen coordination mechanisms (public to public).* Consider consolidating programs in a single document—a consolidated MSME strategy—and outline an action plan with clear objectives and responsibilities of different state bodies in charge of program implementation. • *Encourage proactive involvement* of regional authorities, the private sector, and other relevant institutions (universities, research centers, and the like) to participate in the design and implementation of MSME policies.	Medium term	MNE	Coordination of the large number of stakeholders involved in redesigning and subsequently implementing revised MSME policies may present a major challenge.

Source: World Bank.

Note: MIID = Ministry of Industry and Infrastructural Development; MNE = Ministry of National Economy; MoF = Ministry of Finance; MSMEs = micro, small, and medium enterprises; SMEs = small and medium enterprises; SOEs = state-owned enterprises; TA = technical assistance.

a. Regional akimats are governments of regions, of the capital city, and of cities of significance.

ANNEX 3C: POLICY OPTIONS TO UNLOCK OPPORTUNITIES FOR FOREIGN DIRECT INVESTMENT IN NONEXTRACTIVE SECTORS

TABLE 3C.1 Policy options to unlock opportunities for foreign direct investment in nonextractive sectors

KEY AREAS	PRIORITY	RESPONSIBLE ACTOR(S)	IMPLEMENTATION CHALLENGES
1. Review sector priorities for FDI attraction, identify a small number (three to five) of high-value target sectors for proactive investment promotion that are aligned with Kazakhstan's development objectives in the changing global environment.	Short term	Kazakh Invest, Investment Committee, MFA, MNE	Identifying target sectors would be best done by conducting a sector scan, which would require sector expertise and analytical capacity. The number of entities involved in investment policy and promotion may present a challenge for coordinating and agreeing upon target sectors.
2. Revise the mandate of Kazakh Invest to focus mostly on investment promotion, as well as on policy advocacy and matchmaking between FDI and the local private sector (and not on business regulatory functions).	Short term	Investment Committee, MFA, MNE, Kazakh Invest	Streamlining the mandate of Kazakh Invest will require moving business regulatory functions to another government agency or institution, which will, in turn, need to organize the administration of these additional functions.
3. Introduce key performance indicators to Kazakh Invest for measuring the success of its investment promotion efforts.	Medium term	Investment Committee, MFA, MNE, Kazakh Invest	Introducing key performance indicators will benefit from baseline data and historical information on key targets, which may not be easily accessible.
4. Enhance the governance arrangements for Kazakh Invest by strengthening its board, improving its service contract with the Investment Committee, and ensuring greater consistency of the agency's day-to-day operational management.	Medium term	Investment Committee, MFA, MNE, Kazakh Invest	The number of entities involved in investment promotion may present a challenge for coordinating and agreeing upon reforms to Kazakh Invest's governance.
5. Establish an effective national-subnational framework for coordinating the investment promotion activities of Kazakh Invest and the local-level entities (akimats[a]).	Medium term	Kazakh Invest, akimats, Investment Committee	The capacity of different akimats to undertake investment promotion and facilitation activities may vary greatly, which could result in differing levels of engagement with Kazakh Invest and the need for additional local capacity.
6. Enhance institutional coordination mechanisms between policy makers (ministry) and implementing agencies (Kazakh Invest) of Kazakhstan's investment attraction and retention policies.	Medium term	Investment Committee, MFA, MNE, Kazakh Invest	Having different ministries involved in the policy formulation and implementation, in addition to having a committee under which the investment agency works, means that the development of robust coordination mechanisms or the reorganization of existing reporting structures will be required to create a coherent structure.
7. Assess the current structure and functioning of the Investment Ombudsman and use the analysis to develop a more effective and legally mandated investor grievance mechanism (potentially the "Investment HQ") that is in line with global best practices to avoid costly investor-state disputes.	Medium term	Investment HQ, Prime Minister's Office, MNE	The number of entities involved in investor grievance management may present a challenge for coordinating and agreeing upon the target structure, including a lead agency for grievance management.

Source: World Bank.
Note: FDI = foreign direct investment; MFA = Ministry of Foreign Affairs; MNE = Ministry of National Economy.
a. Regional akimats are governments of regions, of the capital city, and of cities of significance.

ANNEX 3D: POLICY OPTIONS TO BOOST RESEARCH AND DEVELOPMENT AND INNOVATION TO MAXIMIZE THE IMPACT ON PRODUCTIVITY

TABLE 3D.1 Policy options to boost research and development and innovation to maximize the impact on productivity

KEY AREAS	PRIORITY	RESPONSIBLE ACTOR(S)	IMPLEMENTATION CHALLENGES
1. Enhance performance-based public funding and private sector funding of PROs by doing the following: • Improving public financing mechanism to reward higher scientific and commercialization performance of PROs • Introducing incentives to promote contract research at PROs • Improving career incentives for researchers to reward technology commercialization results.	Medium term	MoES and other line ministries (MIID, MoH, MoA, MoE)	The process of introducing competitive funding (through performance-based public funding and private sector funding) of the research might be hampered by the lack of ownership of PRO management because it requires, among other things, reformulating the PRO management structure and PRO management performance evaluation and introducing measurement of the level of cooperation with peer organizations and the private sector.
2. Strengthen the mechanism that ensures merit-based selection of research proposals, specifically by enhancing the engagement of the private sector in formulating research priorities for PROs at the level of national scientific councils.	Short term	MoES and other line ministries (MIID, MoH, MoA, MoE)	Currently, the challenge is to link decisions of national scientific councils to industry needs because there is no real industry interest in the research areas as a result of the lack of dialogue with the private sector.
3. Expand and replicate the innovative consortium activities introduced under the World Bank–financed Fostering Productive Innovation Project.	Short term	MDDIAI	Scaling up the existing consortium grant program may be hampered by the dismantlement of the existing independent selection board and the lack of stable and long-term funding from the public budget.
4. Provide comprehensive technology commercialization support to researchers through the following: • Development of a network of capable technology transfer offices at PROs and universities • Scaling up existing technology commercialization support instruments based on the experience of the Fostering Productive Innovation Project (that is, development of the institute of technology brokers).	Medium term	MoES, MDDIAI	Building up the commercialization capacity of the existing network of technology transfer offices is a key challenge because of the limited knowledge and experience in collaboration with industry and technology commercialization.
5. Develop a mechanism for early-stage financing of start-ups and pipeline-building for later-stage venture investments based on the experience of the Early-Stage Venture Fund under the Fostering Productive Innovation Project.	Medium term	MDDIAI, Baiterek Holding	Funding for early stages of research commercialization (such as the preparation of proofs of concept, prototyping, and the like) is underprovided by the private sector. Therefore, it is important to develop a sound mechanism for early-stage financing. To date, there is not a single early-stage venture capital fund operating in the country.
6. Establish an Innovation Observatory, envisaged under the Fostering Productive Innovation Project, as an efficient science, technology, and innovation policy coordination tool.	Medium term	Prime Minister's Office	The establishment of an independent policy coordinator delineated from multiple interest groups requires strong ownership and leadership by the central government.

Source: World Bank.

Note: MDDIAI = Ministry of Digital Development, Innovation and Aerospace Industry; MFA = Ministry of Foreign Affairs; MIID = Ministry of Industry and Infrastructural Development; MNE = Ministry of National Economy; MoA = Ministry of Agriculture; MoE = Ministry of Energy; MoES = Ministry of Education and Science; MoH = Ministry of Healthcare; PRO = public research organization.

NOTES

1. See Cusolito and Maloney (2018) for an in-depth discussion of the elements of a "national productivity system," the set of policies and institutions necessary to improve the productivity of an economy.
2. Competition is the process of rivalry between suppliers that takes place either in the market or for the market.
3. Mechanisms that affect entry and exit include exclusive rights to supply, limitations on the number of suppliers, or interventions that significantly raise the costs of new firms to enter the market.
4. For instance, through direct restrictions (such as price or product regulation).
5. Dawn raids are unannounced inspections to investigate suspected infringements of competition law.
6. Under the aggregate economywide PMR indicator, each of these two broad pillars—(1) distortions induced by state involvement and (2) barriers to domestic and foreign entry—can be further decomposed into three medium-level indicators that comprise in total 18 low-level indicators.
7. Likewise, and according to Borja, Pop, and Sakhonchik (2021), direct award procurement is still widely used instead of public procurement tenders. The widespread use of direct awards and the concentration of these contracts within a few companies facilitate anticompetitive conduct.
8. Price regulation may be necessary to correct specific market failures—such as natural monopolies or cases of temporary market power arising from external shocks—or to promote certain economic and social protection goals, for instance, granting access to essential goods. However, in competitive markets, or in cases in which government interventions are the cause of limited competition, less distortive alternatives to price regulation should be applied, such as the implementation of competition rules or the elimination of monopoly rights.
9. According to Borja, Pop, and Sakhonchik (2021), the list of food prices regulated by the government of Kazakhstan includes wheat flour of the first grade, wheat bread from first grade flour (molded), horns (weight), buckwheat (unground, weight), polished rice (round grain, weight), and potatoes, among others. According to the Entrepreneurial Code of the Republic of Kazakhstan, apart from the significant food products listed above, the state regulates and approves (1) prices for goods, works, and services in the field of natural monopoly; (2) prices for goods, works, and services produced and sold by the subjects of the state monopoly; (3) prices for the retail sale of petroleum products; (4) maximum prices for medicines; (5) minimum prices for vodka and strong alcoholic beverages; (6) minimum retail prices for cigarettes with and without filters; (7) prices for wholesale of commercial gas in the domestic market of the Republic of Kazakhstan and marginal prices for liquefied petroleum gas sold within the framework of the plan for the supply of liquefied petroleum gas to the domestic market of the Republic of Kazakhstan outside electronic trading platforms; (8) the marginal price of raw and commercial gas purchased by the national operator under the state's preemptive right; (9) tariffs for energy-producing organizations; (10) prices for subsidized services; and (11) prices in socially significant markets.
10. The PMR data can also be organized so as to highlight sector-specific restrictions rather than economywide topics. More specifically, it measures regulatory restrictiveness to competition in network sectors (energy, transport, and e-communications), and other services (retail trade and professional services).
11. According to Van der Marel, Iootty, and Bizhan (2021), the average use of regulated services as a total of all services inputs used in manufacturing production in Kazakhstan is 2.13 percent. The average for upper-middle-income countries is 4.21 percent. According to the methodology used in this study, regulated services are those services for which regulatory information in Kazakhstan is available and comparable across classification schemes. They cover transport and storage, utilities (gas, water), distribution of retail and wholesale, telecommunications, other business services (professional services), and real estate.
12. Kazakhtelecom is the vertically integrated operator in the fixed and mobile telecommunications markets, holding a dominant position in all of them.
13. As discussed in World Bank (Van der Marel, Iootty, and Bizhan 2021), both the sectoral regulator and the antimonopoly regulator are structural units of ministries in charge of

developing the telecommunications sector and economic development in general. This raises concerns about policy interference in regulations. Currently, the telecommunications sector regulatory regime is implemented by the sectoral regulator under the MDDIAI (the Telecommunications Committee) and the Committee on Regulation of Natural Monopolies under the Ministry of National Economy. The fact that both regulators are situated under ministries responsible for policy making on the sectoral and national levels raises concerns about policy interference in regulations.

14. According to World Bank (Van der Marel, Iootty, and Bizhan 2021), although the regulatory framework envisages third-party access to the incumbent Kazakhtelecom's wholesale leased lines, the sector regulator is not proactively applying access procedures. The incumbent Kazakhtelecom owns the legacy infrastructure of communication networks in most urban areas and holds an extremely powerful position in the wholesale access market. Although the regulations require open access to the incumbent's passive network, in practice, private companies often complain about the untransparent and cumbersome process for accessing the essential infrastructure. In particular, access to the incumbent's wholesale leased lines by third-party operators is regulated by the rules on unbundled access to wholesale leased lines, approved by order of the Ministry of Investment and Development in 2016, as well as the model agreement on wholesale leased lines connection (approved by Government Decree No. 709 dated May 14, 2009). Both documents reserve to the incumbent the right to deny access to the wholesale leased lines without technical capacity.

15. Global Connectivity Index database (2020). The index benchmarks 79 countries according to their performance on 40 indicators that track progress in deploying digital infrastructure and capabilities. The database can be accessed at https://www.huawei.com/minisite/gci/en/country-profile-kz.html.

16. Broadband speed for mobile users is relatively low, at an average of 27 megabits per second as of April 2021, leaving Kazakhstan ranked 86th of 134 countries in the 2021 Ookla Global Speedtest Index. In addition, affordability has deteriorated, as reflected in Kazakhstan's rank of 45 in the price subcategory of the 2021 Inclusive Internet Index by the Economist Intelligence Unit, down from the rank of 36 in 2020.

17. As highlighted in Van der Marel, Iootty, and Bizhan (2021), there is no independent infrastructure system operator to guarantee equivalence of access to the rail infrastructure to all rail operators and prevent discrimination.

18. According to recommendations discussed in Borja, Pop, and Sakhonchik (2021), this could be achieved by (1) requiring clear separation between the commercial and noncommercial activities of SOEs, (2) mandating that SOEs earn rates of return comparable to private sector competitors, (3) limiting conflicting roles of the state as regulator and operator in certain sectors, and (4) ensuring full debt and regulatory liability of SOEs.

19. Econometric analysis presented in Van der Marel, Iootty, and Bizhan (2021) shows that removing anticompetitive regulations in services sectors is expected to bring productivity dividends for the downstream economy (manufacturing sector), because final goods producers would be able to get access to cheaper and higher-quality services. The highest payoffs would come from procompetition reforms in rail and road sectors. As for downstream beneficiaries, the largest productivity dividends from procompetition reforms in services sectors would be experienced by food products, chemicals, and basic metals industries. These are typically scale-intensive sectors that can lead to greater diversification of the economy.

20. As highlighted in Van der Marel, Iootty, and Bizhan (2021), in the telecommunications sector, the authorities could consider unbundling the two mobile operators (Mobile Telecom-Service LLP and Kcell JSC), which were originally separate companies, and preparing them for privatization. It could then unbundle Kazakhtelecom JSC into a wholesale and a retail arm to introduce more transparency and eliminate internal cross-subsidies. As for the transport sector, the national railway company is an infrastructure monopoly that both serves the downstream market and provides essential facilities to its downstream competitors, which hampers the entry of private freight transport companies. In this context, the government could consider strengthening vertical separation (in particular, well-enforced accounting separation) between KTZ's operations along the value chain to avoid cross-subsidizing or transfer of funds into segments open to competitors.

21. As discussed in Van der Marel, Iootty, and Bizhan (2021), the telecommunications sector regulatory regime is implemented by a sectoral regulator under the Ministry of Digital Development, Innovation and Aerospace Industry (the Telecommunications Committee), and the regulatory regime in the transport sector is implemented by a sectoral regulator

under the Ministry of Industry and Infrastructural Development (the Transport Committee). The Committee on Regulation of Natural Monopolies is under the Ministry of National Economy in charge of economic development in general. This raises concerns over policy interference in regulation.

22. For example, the incumbent Kazakhtelecom owns the legacy infrastructure of communication networks in most urban areas and holds an extremely powerful position in the wholesale access market. Although the regulations require open access to the incumbent's passive network, in practice, private companies often complain about the untransparent and cumbersome process of accessing the essential infrastructure. In the railway segment, the national railway company operates in the competitive freight-forwarding business but still controls access to an important input of scheduling access to the main railway network. This gives KTZ's freight-forwarding unit access to competitors' sensitive client information. When third parties ask for access to the railway network, KTZ Express can condition the access on managing the client directly (eliminating an intermediary and a competitor). See World Bank (Van der Marel, Iootty, and Bizhan 2021) for further discussion.

23. In particular, the Business Roadmap 2025 program envisages support of private MSMEs in small towns, monotowns, or rural areas and private firms in predefined priority sectors. These sectors include agriculture (plant and cattle farming, fisheries) and related processing (food industry); processing of metals; construction materials; textile and furniture production; machine-building; waste management; transport sector; services with higher value added (information technology, tourism, research and development, and so on); and social services (health, education, sports, and the like). The program's five key indicators are high-level outcome variables (for example, new jobs created, share of SMEs in GDP), while the bulk of intermediate indicators cover provision of working and investment capital as well as partial credit guarantees. The only intermediate indicator that the program explicitly describes as being aimed at increasing firm productivity is "number of external consultants involved in the implementation of new management methods, production technologies, productivity improvement and energy saving of enterprises." All in all, this makes it difficult to attribute productivity growth at the firm level to the program interventions. See Iootty, Bizhan, and Mamrayeva (2021) for further discussion.

24. The electoral program of the Nur Otan party also calls for elaboration of new approaches to entrepreneurship development, including analysis of the efficiency of state support measures; the abolishment of inefficient preferences, subsidies, and state support programs; and further reduction of the SOE footprint in the economy.

25. For instance, the government might consider developing proactive instruments to help MSMEs adapt to new environmental regulations and create, adopt, and sell low-carbon and energy-efficient technologies or services through the development of information-sharing platforms, implementation of green financing mechanisms, and introduction of "green" certification criteria for public procurement purposes. See Iootty, Bizhan, and Mamrayeva (2021) for further discussion.

26. By implementing specific measures to accelerate the adoption of digital technologies by MSMEs (for example, providing one-time marketing consultancy or training vouchers, providing financial support for MSMEs to access cloud computing and purchase cloud technology, promoting awareness campaigns to decrease distrust toward e-commerce practices, and providing comprehensive information and guidelines to MSMEs on regulations related to e-commerce in Kazakhstan and its key trading partners). See Iootty, Bizhan, and Mamrayeva (2021) for further discussion.

27. By strengthening data collection and analytical capacity and broadening the scope of indicators to be monitored. In addition to standard indicators such as disbursement of funds and number of beneficiary firms, it is important to measure intermediate outcomes such as firms reporting new management practices, new production processes, and quality control practices, and performance indicators such as growth in sales (or output), exports, investment, productivity, and so on.

28. As discussed in Iootty, Bizhan, and Mamrayeva (2021), this could be accomplished on two main (parallel) fronts. The first would be to bolster the coordination mechanisms (public to public). The government might consider consolidating programs in a single document—a consolidated SME strategy—and outline an action plan with clear objectives and responsibilities of the different state bodies in charge of program implementation. The second would be to encourage proactive involvement of regional authorities, the private sector,

and other relevant institutions (universities, research centers, and the like) in the design and implementation of MSME policies.

29. National Bank FDI inflow data were only available for the period 2015–18.

30. According to Jedlicka and colleagues' (2021) analysis, the extractives sector has also made up more than 62 percent of announced FDI capital expenditures in Kazakhstan measured in US dollars from 2015 to 2019. According to *FDI Markets*, the share of capital expenditure in the extractives sector has increased compared with previous years. Kazakhstan's concentration of announced FDI capital expenditure in the extractives sector is well above the average for other economies in the Europe and Central Asia region (44 percent in 2015–19), while announced capital expenditure in the services sector is below the region average over the same period (21 percent of announced capital expenditure). Among countries that export significant amounts of oil and gas, Kazakhstan is the only one that has seen a dominant and upward trend in greenfield extractives sector FDI capital expenditures over the period 2005–19.

31. The International Standard Industrial Classification of All Economic Activities (ISIC), Revision 4 classifies activities related to geological prospecting as mining/extractives related.

32. For instance, the establishment of a one-stop shop for investors in Kazakhstan.

33. For example, the 2016 Entrepreneurial Code gives firms and investors more detailed guarantees on the protection of their rights and property. Moreover, the government introduced two business ombudsmen—the Investment Ombudsman and the Commissioner for the Protection of Entrepreneurs' Rights (the Business Ombudsman)—with the objective of supporting companies facing demands for bribes or other forms of unfair treatment and of resolving disputes expeditiously.

34. For instance, the establishment of a specialized judicial board under the Supreme Court for disputes related to the performance of mutual obligations under investment contracts between large investors and government bodies.

35. For example, grant financing programs often have low or no private cofinancing requirements, no requirement to introduce commercialization specialists into the ranks of research groups, and no commercialization key performance indicators. In addition, technology commercialization brokers and private intellectual property specialists in the local market are in short supply, and there are no public programs aimed at addressing these challenges.

36. The term "national innovation system" is used to describe the interactions among institutions, markets, and individuals, comprising a "system." A simplified version of an NIS can be described by three "stakeholders" (government, PROs, and the enterprise sector) and the country's framework conditions needed to initiate, import, modify, and diffuse new technologies and economically useful knowledge.

REFERENCES

Arnold, J., B. Javorcik, M. Lipscomb, and A. Mattoo. 2015. "Services Reform and Manufacturing Performance: Evidence from India." *Economic Journal* 126 (590): 1–39.

Arnold, J. B. Javorcik, and A. Mattoo. 2011. "The Productivity Effects of Services Liberalization: Evidence from the Czech Republic." *Journal of International Economics* 85 (1): 136–46.

Barone, G., and F. Cingano. 2011. "Service Regulation and Growth: Evidence from OECD Countries." *Economic Journal, Royal Economic Society* 121 (555): 931–57.

Baumol, W. J. 1990. "Entrepreneurship: Productive, Unproductive and Destructive." *Journal of Political Economy* 98 (5): 893–921.

Blomström, M., and A. Kokko. 1998. "Multinational Corporations and Spillovers." *Journal of Economic Surveys* 12 (2): 1–31.

Borja C., G. Pop, and A. Sakhonchik. 2021. "Competition, Productivity Growth, and Policy Drivers: An Analysis of Product Market Regulations in Kazakhstan." World Bank, Washington, DC.

Cusolito, A. P., and W. F. Maloney. 2018. *Productivity Revisited: Shifting Paradigms in Analysis and Policy*. Washington, DC: World Bank.

Görg, H., and E. Strobl. 2005. "Spillovers from Foreign Firms through Worker Mobility: An Empirical Investigation." *Scandinavian Journal of Economics* 107 (4): 693–709.

Grover, A., D. Medvedev, and E. Olafsen. 2019. *High-Growth Firms: Facts, Fiction, and Policy Options for Emerging Economies*. Washington, DC: World Bank.

Iootty, M., A. Bizhan, and A. Mamrayeva. 2021. "Policy Options to Support Efficient MSMEs in Kazakhstan." World Bank, Washington, DC.

Jedlicka H., Y. Beksultan, A. Mamrayeva, D. Ojaleye, Z. Rogatschnig, and Y. Sabha. 2021. "FDI Promotion in Kazakhstan: Institutional and Strategic Benchmarking." World Bank, Washington, DC.

Jordaan, J. A., W. Douw, and C. Qiang. 2020. "Multinational Corporation Affiliates, Backward Linkages, and Productivity Spillovers in Developing and Emerging Economies: Evidence and Policy Making." Policy Research Working Paper 9364, World Bank, Washington, DC.

Katila, R. 2000. "Using Patent Data to Measure Innovation Performance." *International Journal of Business Performance Management* 2 (1–3): 180–93.

Katila, R. 2007. "Measuring Innovation Performance." In *Business Performance Measurement*, edited by A. Neely, 304–17. Cambridge, U.K.: Cambridge University Press.

Kenzhaliyev, O., Z. Ilmaliyev, M. Triyono, A. Minghat, M. R. Arpentieva, and G. Kassymova. 2020. "Commercialization of Research and Development Results as the Economy Growth Factor of the Republic of Kazakhstan." *International Journal of Advanced Science and Technology* 29 (7s): 18–28.

Khan, R., and P. Cox. 2017. "Country Culture and National Innovation." *Archives of Business Research* 5 (2). https://doi.org/10.14738/abr.52.2768.

Kitzmueller, M., and M. Licetti. 2012. "Competition Policy: Encouraging Thriving Markets for Development." *Viewpoint*, World Bank Group, Washington, DC.

Kneller, R., and M. Pisu. 2007. "Industrial Linkages and Export Spillovers from FDI." *World Economy* 30 (1): 105–34.

OECD (Organisation for Economic Co-operation and Development). 2021. "Improving the Legal Environment for Business and Investment in Central Asia." Policy Insights Series. OECD, Paris. https://www.oecd.org/eurasia/Improving-LEB-CA-ENG%2020%20April.pdf.

Office of Fair Trading, United Kingdom. 2009. *Government in Markets: Why Competition Matters—A Guide for Policy Makers*. London: Office of Fair Trading.

Poole, J. P. 2013 "Knowledge Transfers from Multinational to Domestic Firms: Evidence from Worker Mobility." *Review of Economics and Statistics* 95 (2): 393–406.

Saurav, A., and R. Kuo. 2020. "A Literature Review on the Effects of FDI on Local Firm Productivity." *World Bank in Focus Note*. World Bank Group, Washington, DC.

Schwab, K., and S. Zahidi. 2020. *The Global Competitiveness Report: How Countries Are Performing on the Road to Recovery*. Geneva: World Economic Forum.

Slavova S., and L. Rubalcaba. 2021. "Unlocking the Potential for Better Business Innovation Performance and Productivity Growth in Kazakhstan." World Bank, Washington, DC.

UNCTAD (United Nations Conference on Trade and Development). 2020. Global Investment Trends Monitor, No. 36. UNCTAD/DIAE/IA/INF/2020/4. UNCTAD, Geneva.

Van der Marel, E., M. Iootty, and A. Bizhan. 2021. "Regulatory Constraints to Competition in Service Sectors in Kazakhstan: Potential Reforms and Productivity Payoffs." World Bank, Washington, DC.

World Bank. 2021. "Enterprise Surveys Follow-Up on COVID-19: Kazakhstan." World Bank Group, Washington, DC.

Zhanbayev, R., S. Sagintayeva, A. Ainur, and A. Nazarov. 2020. "The Use of the Foresight Methods in Developing an Algorithm for Conducting Qualitative Examination of the Research Activities Results on the Example of the Republic of Kazakhstan." *Mathematics* 8 (11): 2024.

www.ingramcontent.com/pod-product-compliance
Lightning Source LLC
Chambersburg PA
CBHW060813270326
41929CB00002B/26